Gospel Poverty
Witness to the Risen Christ

A Study in Biblical Spirituality

Michael D. Guinan, O.F.M.

PAULIST PRESS
New York/Ramsey

Library of Congress
Catalog Card Number 81-80051

ISBN: 0-8091-2377-0

Published by Paulist Press
545 Island Road, Ramsey, N.J. 07446

Printed and bound in the United States of America

CONTENTS

*This book is dedicated to my mother
URSULA GUINAN, who has lived and
taught me many of the values discussed here.*

FOREWORD

by Fr. John Vaughn, O.F.M.
Minister General

This is a book that comes from the heart——the heart of a scholar, teacher, friend, priest, follower of Francis of Assisi. As you follow Michael Guinan's thought, you will relive the history of Israel and discover the richness of the Bible. At the same time you will share in the author's own personal journey in faith. I hope that the book will be for you, as it was for me, an invitation to deepen your faith.

To know what the Bible says (and does not say) about poverty is to be able to understand better Jesus and his mission. It is to come into contact with the tradition in which he grew up; it is to see more clearly what this poverty meant for Jesus, his mother and his apostles; it is to understand better the very spirituality of Jesus. Completely open to and dependent on the Father, he returned *all* in the love of the Spirit.

Jesus, then, is the first Witness. He became poor to give testimony to the Father's love for us. He *became* sin and poverty so that we might become rich in him who is our holiness, our justice and our sanctification. Jesus calls us, in turn, to be witnesses to such love.

Michael Guinan is a warm person and a clear, popular teacher whose scholarship speaks for itself. All of this he has put into a very readable book. May *Gospel Poverty* help us sense better the loveliness of things, and come into contact with the love that created them ——the love that became poor for us.

PREFACE

I have been reflecting on the meaning of Christian poverty for a long time. One can well imagine that in my more than twenty years in the Franciscan Order, the question has arisen from time to time. In 1970, as part of the *resourcement* of the Order, essays treating different aspects of evangelical poverty were commissioned from five top biblical specialists. The papers were first delivered in Rome and then were published, in French, in 1971. In working on my translation of these (see bibliography, *Gospel Poverty*), I came to feel strongly the need for a synthetic presentation of the theme, reflecting the state of contemporary scholarship. Thus I was happy to accept the invitation of Paulist Press to attempt, on a small scale, something of the sort.

Right at the beginning we should note that there is no biblical teaching on poverty; there is a variety of them. One of the characteristics of biblical study today is the recognition of the diversity and plurality within the Bible, a diversity rooted in different times, places and situations in the history of the biblical people. Attempts to reduce the biblical witness to just one aspect (e.g., the *'anawim*) cannot be adequate. The diversity must be recognized and respected, and I have tried to do this.

What I have not tried to do is to relate the biblical teachings directly to issues in our modern world. I freely grant that this is very important, but the space available has limited me to presenting "merely" the biblical data. The reader interested in questions of global hunger, ecological crises and the American role in addressing these issues may consult the fine book by Birch and Rasmussen. J. Murphy O'Connor, O.P. brings his New Testament expertise to bear on questions relative to poverty and religious communities. While hardly mentioning biblical matters, Theodore Roszak's *Person/Planet* critiques modern society from a perspective very much in harmony with the biblical world view. (For all of these, see the bibliography.)

This little book has taken much too long to complete——over two years. The demands of teaching, researching, counseling students and pastoral responsibilities——all requiring attention "right now"—— have made it difficult to find the blocks of time needed to sit down and write. But in a way, the extra time has been helpful. In the first place, it has provided the opportunity to let ideas bat around together, collide, coalesce, and even once in a while jell into some consistent patterns. On the other hand, it has provided the opportunities to develop my thoughts in dialogue and sharing with others. Several of these should be mentioned: the Sisters of Mercy of Burlingame, Calif. for whom I gave renewal workshops in April and May 1976; then, two classes of Franciscan novices at St. Francis Novitiate, Brookline, Mass. where I gave workshops in May 1977 and July 1978; finally, my many colleagues and confreres, but especially Robert J. Karris, O.F.M., Eric Doyle, O.F.M., Francis G. Baur, O.F.M. and John M. Vaughn, O.F.M. Without the discussing, criticizing, and challenging they provided, this book would be quite different.

In the bibliography I have listed some key works which I have found helpful, without implying that I agree with them in all details. In the footnotes, I have tried to provide references to works of a type more popular and more easily available. Many of them contain bibliographies and references to more technical material. Many of them also do not discuss explicitly the questions of riches and poverty, but they do provide the cultural, literary and religious contexts essential to understanding the biblical texts. Biblical quotations are from the New American Bible.

1 BACKGROUND IDEAS

While the problem of riches and poverty is hardly new in the life of the Church, it is posed for us today in an especially acute manner. Pressing social problems within our own country as well as our relationships to other peoples throughout the world make it imperative for us not only to re-examine our individual and collective life styles, but also to face the deeper question of an authentic Christian response to these problems. Briefly put, what does gospel poverty mean for us in our world today?

In the last few years different discussions of the subject have appeared, especially in the area of liberation theology, but few treat the biblical basis of Christian poverty in any adequate way. The biblical data tend to be treated either superficially, as if obvious and well known, or at more length, but in dependence on older and, in some instances, out of date sources. For this reason, a more thorough survey of the state of contemporary biblical scholarship on the question of Christian poverty is in order.

Before we begin our study of the biblical teaching, some preliminary observations are needed. We will discuss first the ambiguous terms "poverty" and "gospel." Some discussion of the role of the Scriptures in our

Gospel Poverty

contemporary situation will follow. Finally, the vocabulary of the poor will be set out.

1. Poverty and Gospel

The word "poverty" can be used in a variety of senses, both positive and negative. Positively, we speak of the virtue of poverty, of gospel poverty, of Christian poverty, of following the poor Jesus. By the end of our study, we will be able to define these uses more closely. Negatively, poverty is the lack of riches in whatever sense these be understood. Since it is thus a relative term (poverty is defined in relation to riches), it is extremely difficult to pin it down in some always valid, objective way.

In a political sense, poverty is the lack of power or ability to influence the political processes. At another level, one may be psychologically or spiritually poor in the sense of lacking psychic, emotional or spiritual resources to cope with life and its problems. Most often though, poverty is understood in its economic sense: the lack of money or material possessions. Here too a range of possibility exists. Socio-economic situations vary considerably from place to place and from time to time, so when we go beyond the minimum level of starving to death, what is poor in one ghetto may be relative comfort in another.

In the ancient world, the basic distinction was between those who worked for their living (the poor) and those who did not (the rich) but lived off property, wealth and the work of others. Those who had nothing were the poorest of the poor.[1]

The term "gospel" is not self-evident either. We speak of the four gospels, of the gospel message, of the gospel at the liturgy. What exactly does "gospel" mean? Essentially there is only one gospel, Jesus Christ. In the person, life and teaching of Jesus, the Father reveals and accomplishes the good news of our salvation. The New Testament preserves four witnesses to this one gospel, *the gospel* according to Matthew, Mark, Luke and John. The rest of the New Testament also bears witness to this Jesus and to what he means. When the New Testament writers came to talk of Jesus, they drew on their Scriptures, the Old Testament, for background, language and insight. Thus the Old Testament too must be studied to deepen our understanding of "the gospel." Nor can we stop there. The experience of the Christian community through the ages has its part to play, and this culminates in our own present world with its needs, problems and questions.

"To live the gospel," then, means to incarnate Jesus in our lives and in our world. "The gospel," Jesus Christ, lives in us and is proclaimed by what we do and say. As we seek to do this authentically, we must take into account the biblical message, the Old and New Testaments, the history and experience of the Christian community through the ages, and our own modern historical and social context. While each of these three areas is important, our study deals only with the first, the biblical message, which has a somewhat unique role to play.

2. The Role of the Scriptures

What role do the Scriptures play in our efforts to live the gospel today? What kind of guidance can we expect to find there? Several easy answers to such questions are available. Some have said, "The Bible was written a long time ago, in ancient languages and cultures. Everything was so different then. The Bible is so timebound that it has nothing to say to us in the modern world." This is not an acceptable option for the Christian. Our tradition has always affirmed that in some way the Scriptures are "canonical," that is, they provide a *kanon* (which is Greek for "measuring stick, ruler") by which we measure ourselves and our progress or lack of progress in the Christian way. Vatican Council II, in its *Decree on Divine Revelation,* continually repeats the need of the Church to root its life and renewal in a profound grasp of the Scriptures. "Like the Christian religion itself, all Church proclamation must feed on, and be ruled by, holy Scripture" (#21).

Another option strongly accepts the authority of the Bible. In seeking guidance on modern problems, it finds passages that seem to deal with the issue and then applies them across the board. This approach, popularly called "fundamentalism," all too casually passes over the time-conditioned questions of ancient language and culture so overstressed by the first approach. In the same Decree noted above, Vatican II also points out and warns us of the difficulties arising from the "human fashion" in which the Scriptures came to be (#12).

Both of these approaches are too simplistic. One neglects the authority of the biblical text in Christian living; the other bypasses the historically conditioned form in which the biblical message comes to us. We are thus faced with a twofold problem: (1) What did the biblical text mean when it was set down? (2) How do we apply this today? Needless to say, this is a very complex problem which we can only touch on here.

What kind of guidance can we expect to find in the Scriptures? Minimally, we can say that we will not find a new code of laws or a list of "do's" and "don'ts." Nor can we expect detailed answers to our modern moral and social problems; circumstances and cultures change too much and too fast for that. Broadly speaking, we can expect to find two kinds of guidelines: negative and positive. Negatively, biblical teaching may rule out some kinds of behavior as incompatible with life in God's kingdom. Positively, goals and ideals, directions and attitudes are presented which Christians must always keep in focus. An example: as difficult as it may be to determine in the concrete here and now the specific way of living Jesus' teaching on love, we are sure that hatred has no place, and this includes "holy hatred" of God's enemies.[2]

3. The Vocabulary of the Poor

Generally speaking, the Bible deals less with abstract concepts and more with concrete situations. It should not be surprising then to find less talk of "poverty" and more of "the poor." The best known and most popular biblical word for "the poor" is *'anawim.* The *'anawim* are, in fact, on the way to becoming a cliché in some theological and spiritual writing. The basic meaning of the Hebrew word is still under discussion, but its usage indicates situations of social inferiority, especially oppression.

Biblical data on the poor is, however, much more extensive than texts dealing with the *'anawim.* Other important terms occur. Among these are *'ebyon* (one who is poor and must beg); *dal* (one weak or feeble, in both a social and a physical sense); *rash* (one needy or deprived). In Greek a similar range of terms exists.

"This vocabulary expresses an understanding of poverty quite different from our own. For our modern languages, as already in Greek and Latin, poverty is the lack of goods; it is an economic idea. While Hebrew sometimes considers poverty a lack ... or a situation of begging ... it views it primarily as a situation of dependence ... or weakness.... In the biblical mind, the poor person is less one who is indigent and more one who is oppressed, an inferior or a lesser one. It is a social idea."[3]

2 THE BIBLE AND THE WORLD

When we speak about poverty and material things, our attitude to the whole of material creation comes into play. How do we view, how do we evaluate the material world in general? On this point, most of the modern Western world differs considerably from the biblical point of view.[1]

The tone of the biblical view of the world is set in Genesis 1. Over and over again in the course of this chapter, the refrain is heard: God saw how good it was. In the mythologies of the ancient world, evil, sin and disorder are built into the structure of the world, a structure which reflects strife and conflict in the world of the gods. But in the Bible, this is not the case. The world is good because its one creator is good. Human sin can mess things up, but the underlying fact remains: God saw how good it was.

Human beings live firmly rooted in this world. We are formed from the clay of the ground (Gen 2:7), and at death we return to the ground (Gen 3:19). We are one matter with creation. To live, in a full sense, involves sharing in some degree in the good things of the earth; material things are involved. If we lack food, shelter, clothing, etc., something important is missing from human life. Living in harmony with God, the source of life, is thought, naturally and normally, to bring with it a share in the good things of the earth (e.g., Dt 28:1–14). Sometimes this is called "pragmatism" or "utilitarianism," but such an evaluation fails completely to appreciate the underlying world view of the Bible. If a person is living in destitution or oppression, something is missing in his or her relationship to the world. Something is wrong somewhere, and the Bible has a definite idea what to call it: sin.

The strong unity between humankind and natural creation is brought out in the context of sin, of disunity. Because of human sin, the soil itself shares in a curse (Gen 3:17); because of human sin, the whole world returns to primordial chaos (Gen 6:12; 7:11). A similar thought is found in Isaiah 24:4–5:

> The earth mourns and fades,
>   the world languishes and fades;
>   both heaven and earth languish.
> The earth is polluted because of its inhabitants,
>   who have transgressed laws, violated statutes,
>   broken the ancient covenant.

The point is clear: human sin, injustice, turning from God threaten the very structure of the world. There is no such thing as a private or solitary sin. We are all in this together.

This same basic approach appears in the New Testament. Jesus taught by way of parables. Whenever a woman works with yeast making bread, the kingdom of God is there (Lk 13:20–21); when fishermen throw their nets into the sea, the kingdom of God is there (Mt 13:47–50). In the world, where we live, in all these human situations, the kingdom of God is there. The parables are not just nice little stories to help us think of God. They show us how God's revelation and presence come to us: in and through the world of nature and of human society.

The whole world was created in and through Christ (Jn 1:1–4; Col 1:15–20), and all of creation is involved in his work. Just as we ourselves do, so all of creation groans, awaiting the fullness of redemption (Rom 8:19–23). In the life of the Church, we can see how material things—bread, wine, water, oil—have already begun to be transformed by the presence of Christ.

The Bible then has a view of the world which is basically positive, and a view of human existence in the world which is essentially participatory. The modern Western world sees things differently. I am here; everyone and everything else stand over there. My relationship to them is largely antagonistic. I relate to things and to people in a competitive, aggressive, domineering way. Religiously speaking, material things can separate me from God; I have to struggle against them. Do I choose God or things?

This is a very unbiblical approach. For the biblical person, only sin separates one from God. I live immersed in the world. The choice is not "things or God," but rather "me-and-things-with-God" or "me-and-things-without-God." We are not "over-against"; we are "part of" the world and material things.

Throughout its history, the Church has faced world-denying impulses. Influenced often by dualistic thought with its strong matter-spirit dichotomy, movements such as Gnosticism, Manichaeism, Albigensianism, and Jansenism have infected our theology and spirituality. Official Christianity has always rejected these as being incompatible with biblical revelation. It would be foolish to suggest that these movements belong only to the past and today we can relax our guard against them. Any approach to Gospel poverty, to a Christian attitude toward material things, must hold closely to the biblical view of material creation and of our relationship to it.

3 EXODUS AND SINAI

1. Exodus and Deliverance

In the mid-second millennium B.C., because of famine in Canaan, a group of Hebrew clans came to Egypt in search of food and pasturage. They found both and settled in Egypt in the delta region. With the rise of a new, native Egyptian dynasty, these settled Semites were perceived as a foreign group, and they experienced oppression and enslavement at the hands of the ruling power. When the Pharaoh, Ramesses II came to the throne (1290-1224 B.C.), they were put to work on his extensive building operations. "Still the Israelites groaned and cried out because of their slavery. As their cry for release went up to God, he heard their groaning and was mindful of his covenant with Abraham, Isaac and Jacob. He saw the Israelites and knew. . . . " (Ex 2:23-25).

God called Moses to free his people from their oppression and to lead them into the desert to worship him (Ex 4:23; 5:1; etc.). They left in haste and were pursued by the Egyptian force. At a body of water (called in Hebrew the "sea of reeds"), they faced certain death at the hands of their pursuers, but then something happened. Yahweh, their God, delivered them "by his mighty hand and outstretched arm" (cf. Dt 11:2). The Hebrews were snatched from death and blessed with new life; the Egyptians were drowned in the sea. This was the greatest of Yahweh's saving deeds for his people and formed one of the central affirmations of Israel's faith. "I am Yahweh, your God who brought you out from the land of Egypt, that place of slavery" (Ex 20:2; Dt 5:6).

2. Sinai and Covenant

Like any major event in one's life, it would take time to assimilate this great act of Yahweh. The Hebrews did not realize at first the various dimensions of what had happened. They came to Sinai, and there, under Moses' leadership, began to understand something of the meaning of what they had experienced during the exodus.

Their first realization related to Yahweh. They came to see that he had acted as their kinsman. He had freely bound himself to them and had accepted them as his relatives, his kin, so to speak. Within the tribal structure of Israel, certain kinsmen had the obligation to step in and protect weaker members of the tribe, or to recover property stolen from the tribe, or to free members of the tribe enslaved by enemies. These persons were called "the *go'el*" ("redeemer" or "recoverer") (e.g., Lev 25:25, 47–49; Jer 32:6–7; etc.). As a faithful kinsman, Yahweh had assumed the role of *go'el* and redeemed the Israelites from slavery and the bondage of Egypt (e.g., Ex 15:13).[2]

If Yahweh was their kin, then they were his family, his people (e.g., Ex 6:7). A ritual was performed which expressed this relationship: a covenant was sealed. Exodus 24 describes a blood ritual (vv. 6-8) and a meal (vv. 5, 11). Both of these express the same reality:

Yahweh and the Israelites formed one people sharing one life. For the Israelites, the blood signified life (Lev 17:11) and a meal represented one family together nourishing and sharing its life.

Another realization followed. They were one family with Yahweh: they shared life with their God. And what do you do with a life but live it? The covenant with Yahweh must make a difference in their behavior. Covenant involves obligation. In fact, two kinds of obligations flow: one affecting their relation to Yahweh, and one their relation to other people.

Yahweh's deliverance of Israel from Egypt was not just a freedom *from;* it was also a freedom *for:* "Let my son (Israel) go that he may serve me" (Ex 4:23). Israel's first duty was to be faithful to Yahweh. This is spelled out clearly in the first commandment. "I am the Lord your God who brought you out of the land of Egypt, out of the house of bondage. You shall have no other gods before me" (Ex 20:2–3). The Hebrew word for "bondage" and "slavery" is related to the words for "servant" and for "service, worship." When they were in Egypt, they were "slaves/servants" of Pharaoh; now they are "servants" of Yahweh and owe "service/worship" to him alone (Lev 25:42, 55). The god we worship is the ultimate source of our values and behavior. The great sin against the covenant is idolatry, worshiping false gods (e.g., Dt 13). The Israelites must "serve" only Yahweh and seek to "be holy, for I, the Lord, your God am holy" (Lev 19:2).

In striving to "be holy," the Israelites came to know that they also had an obligation in relation to other people. In delivering them from Egypt, Yahweh had acted as a kinsman, taking social obligation seriously. If they were to live as true servants of this

Yahweh, the Israelites too must take social obligation seriously. In fact, we find in the Pentateuch a great deal of legal material touching on all areas of life with others. Especially prominent here is the way in which the Israelites are to act vis-à-vis the poor, the oppressed, the aliens (who lived in the land without any legal rights or recourse). They had been poor and oppressed and aliens in the land of Egypt, and Yahweh had delivered them. When they are commanded not to oppress others, this motivation is frequently expressed: "because you were once strangers (aliens) in the land of Egypt" (e.g., Ex 22:21; 23:9; Lev 19:34; Dt 10:18; 14:28–29; 15:1ff, etc.). It would be the grossest contradiction for the redeemed people of God to become themselves oppressors of the poor.

In Exodus 24, the laws and obligations precede the sealing of the covenant. The people cry out, "All that the Lord has said, we will heed and do" (24:7). They commit themselves to the covenant fully aware of the obligations involved. While the biblical text itself does not do so, popular understanding of the ten commandments (Ex 20:1–17; Dt 5:6–21) has divided them into the commandments of the first tablet, which relate to God, and those of the second tablet, which relate to neighbor. The two areas are in fact intimately tied together; if the Israelites really serve Yahweh, this will show up in the way they treat others. To become oppressors of the poor and needy is to reverse the meaning of the exodus and the covenant.

3. Conclusions

1. Poverty and oppression are evils. In their distress and helplessness, the poor cry to Yahweh for deliverance.

2. Yahweh is a God who hears and delivers from poverty and oppression and helplessness.

3. The Hebrews realize that they must worship and serve this Yahweh alone. The whole purpose of the liberation from Egypt was precisely to become servants of Yahweh. We recall the old spiritual, "Tell ol' Pharaoh, let my people go!" This, however, is only half of the sentence; it continues, "so that they might serve me" (e.g., Ex 7:16). The covenant at Sinai, this whole new way of living, is the goal of the liberation from Egypt. The Israelites would be truly free only if and when they lived their covenant with Yahweh.

4. As members of God's covenant people, the Israelites must also treat others justly. If they really live the covenant and worship Yahweh, they will not deal unjustly with others, will not oppress others.

Of course, when they settle in the land, things will change.

4 ROYAL THEOLOGY AND THE WORDS OF THE WISE

About 1200 B.C., the Israelite tribes were settled in the land of Canaan and lived a fairly independent existence for about two hundred years. Then a big change took place. The continuing threat posed by the presence of the Philistines, a non-Semitic people living along the western plain, highlighted the need for a stronger sort of government and defense. The loosely organized tribes were no longer able to meet the situation; they asked for a king (1 Sam 8:1–9). Despite warnings and opposition, the people persisted, "There must be a king over us. We too must be like the other nations, with a king to rule us and to lead us in warfare and fight our battles" (1 Sam 8:19b–20). Saul was anointed king first (1 Sam 9–10), but was later replaced by David (1 Sam 16:1–13) who gradually consolidated his power and established his rule in Jerusalem.

1. Royal Theology

The period of the monarchy had begun, and this represented not only a major social reorganization but also a serious religious crisis (e.g., 1 Sam 8:6–8). What exactly was the problem? Kingship did not simply drop into Israel out of the blue. It was an old institution in the ancient Near East and with it came a great deal of ideological baggage. A whole religious mythology was associated with kingship, and when the Israelites adopted the political forms, great danger existed of taking the mythology over along with it.[1] They would then cease being true Yahwists and would indeed become a nation like all the rest.

The king was basically the guardian of the stability of the cosmos.[2] If the king was a healthy and a good king, society and creation were in order; if he was a poor king, or was ill and unable to exercise kingly functions, then chaos threatened. Each year a New Year's festival was celebrated when the creation mythology would be recited and re-enacted in the liturgy, and at the conclusion, having defeated the forces of chaos, Marduk (in Babylon) or Ba'al (in Canaan) was proclaimed king, and creation was stablized for another year. The earthly king was the representative of the gods and played a role in the celebration. Kingship and creation were closely tied together.

As king or, better, kingpin of creation, the ruler had the obligation particularly of maintaining justice in the realm. Injustice is a form of dis-order, of chaos, and flows from the failure of kingship. One scholar has recently maintained that the word often translated "justice" *(sedaqa)* in fact means "world order."[3] This concern of the king for justice occurs throughout the Near East. From Mesopotamia, a clear example can be found in the famous Code of Hammurabi:

> At that time Anum and Enlil (Babylonian gods)
>   named me
> to promote the welfare of the people

me, Hammurabi, the devout, god-fearing prince,
to cause justice to prevail in the land,
to destroy the wicked and the evil,
that the strong might not oppress the weak. . . .

In my bosom I carried the peoples of the land
    of Sumer and Akkad;
they prospered under my protection;
I always governed them in peace,
I sheltered them in my wisdom
in order that the strong might not oppress the
    weak,
that justice might be dealt the orphan and the
    widow. . . . [4]

The widow and the orphan are mentioned expressly because they were the weakest and most defenseless members of the society and, hence, most likely to suffer injustice. The rich and the powerful could well take care of themselves.

From Canaan, the story of King Keret (or Kirta) shows the same concern. Keret is lying sick in bed. His son, desiring to replace him on the throne, comes in and tells him to come down from the throne. Because Keret is unable to exercise his kingship, the society is threatened by invasion from without and by injustice from within:

Listen, Kirta the Noble,
    listen closely and pay attention:
as though raiders had raided, you will be driven out,
    and forced to live in the mountains.
Weakness has stayed your hand:
    you do not judge the cases of widows,

you do not preside over the hearings of the
     oppressed;
you do not drive out those who plunder the poor,
     you do not feed the orphan before you,
     the widow behind your back.[5]

This general ideology of kingship appeared throughout
the ancient world: the king must maintain world order,
and a key part of this is justice in the social order.

So the Israelites got a king, and, as we can well
imagine, there were tensions with the religious traditions of Yahweh who had freed them from Egypt
and covenanted with them at Sinai. In taking over kingship, it had to remain very clear that Yahweh alone
was head over Israel. Kingship in Israel was validated
in at least two ways: (1) through the concepts of promise and fulfillment extending through the patriarchal
and Sinai stories, the king was seen as willed and in-
tended by Yahweh;[6] (2) the kingship of David was based
on a new word from Yahweh, spoken through his
prophet Nathan (2 Sam 7). Yahweh had made a covenant with David and his family.[7] In the oracle of Nathan, it is made very clear that Yahweh and Yahweh
alone is the source of David's greatness and power,
and that David must obey Yahweh's will ("If he does
wrong, I will correct him"—2 Sam 7:14). In speaking
of their king, Israel will make use of creation language
and borrow some of the ideas of kingship, but the
king is squarely under Yahweh's law (e.g., Dt 17:14–
20). Yahweh is king of Israel.

As we might expect, one of the key concerns of
Yahweh and his representative, the king, is justice in
the realm, putting an end to the oppression of the
poor and needy. This concern will appear in different

parts of the Old Testament, e.g., the Book of Proverbs, the psalms, and the prophets (as we shall see later):

By justice a king gives stability to the land (Pr 29:4a).

If a king is zealous for the rights of the poor
    his throne stands firm forever (Pr 29:14).

It is not for kings to drink wine;
    strong drink is not for princes!
Lest in drinking they forget what the law decrees,
    and violate the rights of all who are in need. . . .
Open your mouth, decree what is just,
    defend the needy and the poor (Pr 31:4–5, 9).

Sing praise to the Lord enthroned in Zion. . ..
He has not forgotten the cry of the afflicted
    (Ps 9:12–13).

Rise, O Lord! O God, lift up your hand!
    Forget not the afflicted. . . .
On you the unfortunate man depends;
    of the fatherless, you are the helper. . . .
The Lord is king forever and ever. . . .
    The desire of the afflicted you hear, O Lord
        (Ps 10:12, 14, 16, 17).

Yahweh is king in Israel and his kingdom should be one of justice and mercy. The human king is Yahweh's representative and should rule in such a way that Yahweh's kingdom may be seen for what it truly is. The Israelites already knew Yahweh as the God who freed them from the slavery and oppression of Egypt and whose concern for social justice found expression in the covenant of Sinai. Yahweh's covenant with David would continue and deepen this concern for justice in the realm.

2. The Words of the Wise

In the quotation above from the Code of Hammurabi, we saw the Babylonian king claiming, "I sheltered them in my wisdom." If the king was to rule well, he was to rule wisely. In the Old Testament, the connection between ruling and wisdom is often made, but it is especially clear in the case of Solomon who became renowned for his wisdom (1 Kgs 3; 5:9–14). Besides the king, advisors, counselors, judges, scribes, etc. were needed for the smooth functioning of the court and temple. Well-off, upper class "intellectuals" were present too in the society in general.[8]

From circles such as these, the wisdom literature of the Old Testament was produced (i.e., Proverbs, Job, Qoheleth (Ecclesiastes), Ben Sira (Ecclesiasticus), Wisdom of Solomon, and other smaller works). In addition to a common social background, they share the wisdom approach to life, an approach which found the presence of God through observation and reflection on the ordinary, day-to-day facts of experience.[9] Even a cursory glance through this literature shows a concern for questions of riches and poverty.

First of all, we can note a series of simple observations on the poor and the rich. These give no value judgments or teachings; they merely record experience:

The rich man's wealth is his strong city;
    the ruination of the lowly is their poverty (Pr 10:15).

One man is lavish, yet grows still richer;
> another is too sparing, yet is the poorer
>> (Pr 11:24).

One man pretends to be rich, yet has nothing;
> another pretends to be poor, yet has great wealth
>> (Pr 13:7).

Even by his neighbor the poor man is hated,
> but the friends of the rich are many (Pr 14:20).

See also 18:23; 19:4, 7; 22:7.

Second, many proverbs warn against laziness, idle talk and carousing in general; all of these lead to poverty. On the other hand rising early, working hard, and being diligent all lead to wealth. The well-off wise are training their children in good work habits.

The slack hand impoverishes,
> but the hand of the diligent enriches (Pr 10:4).

Laziness plunges a man into deep sleep,
> and the sluggard must go hungry (Pr 19:15).

In all labor there is profit,
> but mere talk tends only to penury (Pr 14:23).

See also 13:18; 20:13; 21:17; 23:20; 24:30–34 (cf. 6:6–11); 28:19; 29:3; etc. Riches then are the fruit of diligence and hard work; poverty is the fruit of laziness.

Third, from here it was an easy step to see riches as the reward from God for living wisely and justly, and poverty as the divine punishment for foolishness and sin. Thus riches and poverty come to carry religious and moral meaning.

Honor the Lord with your wealth,
     with first fruits of all your produce;
Then will your barns be filled with grain,
     with new wine your vats will overflow (Pr 3:9–10).

Long life is in her (i.e., wisdom's) right hand,
     in her left are riches and honor (Pr 3:16).

See also 8:17–21; Psalm 112; etc. A similar evaluation, perhaps under wisdom influence, appears throughout Deuteronomy. Faithfulness to the Mosaic Torah leads to life, prosperity, etc. (cf. Dt 6:1–3, 10–15; 28:1–69).

In approaching these texts, however, two things should be borne in mind. (1) This does not represent simply a crass pragmatism: if you want to become rich, just be good. We have to recall the Hebraic view of the world that we discussed above. Living in harmony with God had to overflow and affect all levels of one's existence, with others and with nature. If some material comfort was lacking, there was disharmony somewhere. (2) We run across Proverbs such as these:

Sometimes a way seems right to a man,
     but the end of it leads to death
          (Pr 14:12/16:25).

Man may make plans in his heart,
     but what the tongue utters is from the Lord
          (Pr 16:1).

See also 16:2, 9; 19:21; 20:24; 21:30–31; etc. The sages clearly recognized that things did not always turn out the way they should. There are limits to what we can know and explain. Such limits have a name, Yahweh. As time went on, however, in some circles these limits were overlooked, and a rigid dogmatism resulted: if you are poor and suffering, then you must have sinned. The Book of Job is a cry of anguish protesting such arrogant certainty.

Fourth, the well-off wise recognized that things were really more complex than that. Two things stand out:

(1) Riches are not the ultimate value; there are things in life which are more important.

Wealth is useless on the day of wrath,
　　but virtue saves from death (Pr 11:4).

He who trusts in his riches will fall,
　　but like green leaves the just flourish (Pr 11:28).

Better a little with fear of the Lord
　　than a great fortune with anxiety (Pr 15:16).

From a man's greed comes his shame;
　　rather be a poor man than a liar (Pr 19:22).

See also 1:8–19; 12:9; 17:1; 19:1; 20:21; 22:1; 23:4–5; 28:6; 29:7; Sirach 29:22. Virtue, justice, fear of the Lord—all are more basic and more important than riches. If it comes to a choice, they should prevail.

(2) Those who are well off have the obligation of not oppressing the poor and of giving alms to alleviate their poverty.

He who sins despises the hungry;
>   but happy is he who is kind to the poor
>   (Pr 14:21).

He who oppresses the poor blasphemes his Maker,
>   but he who is kind to the needy glorifies him
>   (Pr 14:31).

He who has compassion on the poor lends to the
>   Lord,
>   and he will repay him for his good deed
>   (Pr 19:17).

Injure not the poor because they are poor,
>   nor crush the needy at the gate;
For the Lord will defend their cause,
>   and will plunder the lives of those who
>   plunder them (Pr 22:22–23).

See also 17:5; 21:13; 22:9, 16; 28:3, 27; 29:7, 13; Job 31:16ff; Sirach 4:1–10; Psalm 112:9; etc. One thing should be noted here. We saw above that the Sinai covenant contains strong injunctions not to oppress the poor. The motivation frequently cited ("because you were once slaves in Egypt") appealed to the memory of the exodus and God's redeeming activity. Here, in the wisdom material, the motivation is different. The appeal is to the recognition of the common Creator who is concerned for justice in the world.

The balance of the reflections of the wise is well summed up in Proverbs 30:7–9:

Two things I ask of you,
>   deny them not to me before I die:

> Put falsehood and lying far from me,
>> give me neither poverty nor riches;
>> (provide me only with the food I need;)
> Lest, being full, I deny you,
>> saying, "Who is the Lord?"
> Or, being in want, I steal,
>> and profane the name of my God.

Riches are a great danger; they lead to arrogance and setting oneself up without Yahweh: "I have everything. Who needs God?" Ben Sira stresses the same point: "For the sake of profit many sin" (Sir 27:1–2); "The lover of gold will not be free from sin" (Sir 31:5). In fact, a rich man without fault is nothing short of miraculous (Sir 31:8–11). On the other hand, poverty reduces to destitution and leads to stealing and breaking Yahweh's commandments. Extreme poverty and extreme wealth both have their problems in leading us away from Yahweh. The words of the wise recognize and warn against them.

3. Conclusions

1. Royal theology and wisdom theology go hand in hand with creation theology and are concerned for order and justice in the world. This perspective differs significantly from that of the theology of God's saving activity at the exodus and Sinai.[10]

2. Exodus-Sinai, as we saw, begins from a position of weakness, of need, of oppression. Royal and wisdom thought begins from a position of power, of strength, of responsibility. If the former is a theology of "have-nots," the latter speaks to the "haves."[11]

3. In Israel, Yahweh is the king; the human ruler

is his representative who must live under his law and reflect his rule of justice, mercy and love, a rule which shows itself especially in concern for the poor, the helpless and the oppressed.

4. The wise, reflecting an upper class background, regard riches as the reward of justice and hard work, and poverty as the fruit of laziness and folly. But they also recognize the danger and relativity of riches. Fear of the Lord is more basic and more important. As children of the one Creator, the wealthy must not oppress the weak, and they must alleviate poverty by sharing what they possess.

5 THE PROPHETS AND THE POOR

We have seen two different theological perspectives in ancient Israel, one coming to expression in the Mosaic, Sinai covenant, the other in the Davidic, Jerusalem covenant. Both had a strong sense of justice for the poor and the oppressed, and both could be violated. When this happened, Yahweh raised up spokesmen to call the people and the king back to covenant fidelity. When a response was not forthcoming, punishment from the Lord was threatened: the northern kingdom of Israel was destroyed by Assyria in 722 B.C., and the southern kingdom of Judah fell to Babylon in 587 B.C.

The prophets (in Hebrew, *nabi*, "one sent"), sent by God to speak his word to the people, appear especially during the period of the monarchy. We saw above the prophet Nathan proclaiming God's covenant with David and his family (2 Sam 7). A short time later, David violates his neighbor's wife, Bathsheba, and has Uriah, her husband, killed. Nathan strongly reprimands David, who is punished and repents of his sin (2 Sam 11:1–12:24). Prophets appear at other times throughout the monarchy, and we cannot here look at each of them in detail.[1] We will focus instead on three: Elijah, Amos and Isaiah.

1. Elijah

Elijah appears on the scene in the northern kingdom during the reign of Ahab and his Canaanite wife, Jezebel (869–850 B.C.). We do not have any oracles from Elijah, but, rather, stories about him, all of which deal, in one way or another, with the clash between Yahwism and Canaanite Baalism. The story of particular interest for our theme occurs in 1 Kings 21, the story of Naboth's vineyard.[2]

Ahab, the king, desires Naboth's vineyard to use as a garden, but the latter staunchly refuses to give it to him. It is part of Naboth's family inheritance from the Lord. Ahab realizes that Naboth's claim is sound; even as king, he is limited by Yahweh's law, so he goes back to his palace to sulk. His wife, Jezebel, chides him for giving in; as a Canaanite, she knows no limitations on kingship. She arranges not only to get the vineyard but also to have Naboth killed in the process. Elijah encounters the king and sharply rebukes him. Ahab admits his guilt and does penance, fasting and wearing sackcloth. He knows that the covenant with Yahweh puts limits on his kingship and that he has violated these. Elijah calls him back to the social justice which is part of the Mosaic covenant.

2. Amos

The first of the so-called "writing" prophets is Amos, who preached in the northern kingdom about a century after Elijah, ca. 750 B.C. The gross violation of social justice is a recurring theme.[3]

Thus says the Lord:
> For three crimes of Israel and for four,
> I will not revoke my word;

Because they sell the just man for silver,
> and the poor man for a pair of sandals.
They trample the heads of the weak into the dust of
> the earth,
> and force the lowly out of the way (2:6–7).

Hear this word, women of the mountain of Samaria,
> you cows of Bashan,
You who oppress the weak
> and abuse the needy;
Who say to your lords,
> "Bring drink for us" (4:1).

Yes, I know how many are your crimes,
> how grievous your sins:
Oppressing the just, accepting bribes,
> repelling the needy at the gate (5:12).

Hear this, you who trample upon the needy
> and destroy the poor in the land!
"When will the new moon be over," you ask,
> "that we may sell our grain,
> and the sabbath, that we may display the wheat?
We will diminish the ephah, add to the shekel
> and fix our scales for cheating!
We will buy the lowly man for silver,
> and the poor man for a pair of sandals;
> even the refuse of the wheat we will sell!"
> > (8:4–6).

These flagrant violations of the covenant are rooted in false worship. The Israelites have forsaken Yahweh and gone after pagan gods (e.g., 4:4–5; 5:4–6; 5:26; etc.). Idolatry is the basic sin which finds expression in social injustice. Amos urged them to leave their sin and return to Yahweh, their God. "Yet you returned not to me, says the Lord" (4:6, 8, 9, 10, 11). The northern kingdom fell to Assyria approximately one generation later, in 722 B.C.

3. Isaiah

After the fall of the north, a series of prophets spoke Yahweh's word to Judah in the south, e.g., Micah, Isaiah, Jeremiah, and others. Here we will look only at Isaiah.[4]

Isaiah seems to have been a well-educated person with ties at the royal court. He received his call in the Jerusalem temple (6:1–9) and had frequent access to the king. It is not surprising to find him speaking strongly in the context of Davidic covenant thought.[5] Within this context, Isaiah does not hesitate to excoriate the king and princes for failing to establish right and justice in the realm. He tells them:

Put away your misdeeds from before my eyes;
    cease doing evil; learn to do good.
Make justice your aim; redress the wronged,
    hear the orphan's plea, defend the widow
        (1:16–17).

Your princes are rebels and comrades of thieves;
    each one of them loves a bribe and looks for gifts.
The fatherless they defend not,
    and the widow's plea does not reach them (1:23).

The Lord enters into judgment
    with his people's elders and princes:

It is you who have devoured the vineyard;
    the loot wrested from the poor is in your house.
What do you mean by crushing my people,
    and grinding down the poor when they look to
        you?
    says the Lord, the God of hosts (3:14–15).

See also 5:23–24; 10:1–4; 14:30, 32; etc.

The kings have not been true representatives of
Yahweh; they have not established right and justice
in the kingdom. Isaiah talks of a future descendant
of David, an anointed king (Hebrew: *messiah*), who will
rule wisely and justly:

For a child is born to us, a son is given us;
    upon his shoulders dominion rests.
They name him Wonder-Counselor, God-Hero
    Father-Forever, Prince of Peace.
His dominion is vast
    and forever peaceful,
From David's throne and over his kingdom,
    which he confirms and sustains
By judgment and justice,
    both now and forever.
The zeal of the Lord of hosts will do this (9:5–6).

But a shoot shall sprout from the stump of Jesse,
    and from his roots a bud shall blossom.
The spirit of the Lord shall rest upon him:
    a spirit of wisdom and of understanding,
A spirit of counsel and of strength,
        a spirit of knowledge and of fear of the Lord,
        and his delight shall be the fear of the Lord.

Not by appearance shall he judge,
   nor by hearsay shall he decide.
But he shall judge the poor with justice
   and decide aright for the land's afflicted
     (11:1–4).

While they had not seen a king who really did justice, there will be one; Yahweh is faithful to his promises. It is likely that Isaiah may have been thinking of the next king, Hezekiah, but these oracles of justice and peace, hope and promise would not be forgotten. As its messianic hope grew, later Judaism would recall them.

4. Conclusions

1. Both the Mosaic and the Davidic covenants strongly stressed the obligation not to oppress the poor and to deal justly with all. Both covenants were violated.

2. When this happened, God sent his spokesmen, the prophets, to call the people and the king back to covenant fidelity.

3. For the prophets, the cause of poverty and oppression was found in forsaking the covenant, be it Mosaic or Davidic. The solution will be found in returning to the covenant, in both of its dimensions.

4. Mistreatment of others flows from worshiping false gods. The prophets speak out against idolatry, forsaking the Lord, and against the form in which this manifests itself toward others: social injustice. The prophets do not say a great deal to the poor; they speak primarily to the oppressors, those in and with power, those who can make a difference.[6]

5. If the Israelites do not return to the covenant, the prophets threaten punishment. Israel, the northern kingdom, is destroyed by Assyria; Judah in the south falls to Babylon and goes into exile.

6 THE POOR AND THE PIOUS

1. The Exile and Its Problems

In 587 B.C., the Babylonians, tired of the recurring problems in Judea, destroyed Jerusalem, its palace and temple. Those left in the land were poor, dispirited and exposed to harassment by the neighboring peoples. The king and the upper classes were deported to Babylon. If the establishment of the monarchy more than four hundred years before had occasioned a religious crisis, its destruction was even more shattering. The Judean community had a great deal of soul-searching to do. They came to realize two basic things: (1) what they were experiencing was a covenant curse on covenant disobedience (Dt 28:15–69); they had forsaken Yahweh. At the same time, (2) they believed that Yahweh was faithful to his promises, and this was the basis for their hope.[1]

In 539 B.C., the Persians wrested power from the Babylonians and allowed the conquered peoples to return to their homes. They were permitted their religious practices and some independence, but no nationalist revivals were tolerated. This presented problems. Who would be in charge of the community returning to Judea? What vision would animate them? Several different groups were in contention. The royalists, of course, the king's party, had hopes of restoring

a successor to David. The last such we hear of is Zer-
ubabel (Ezra 4:8f) who passes quietly from the scene.
The "messianic" hope will become more spiritualized
(e.g., in the Chronicler's history, David is a strongly
religious leader) and will go underground, emerging
later in the hope that God will bring in his kingdom.
The prophets, especially the followers of Second Isaiah,
looked forward to a cosmic future when Yahweh would
intervene to defeat his enemies. The priestly group
looked, instead, backward, to the time before the mon-
arch, to the Mosaic period, and saw in the Mosaic law
a blueprint for the future. In fact, the priests wind
up with the leadership, and the Torah, the Law of
Moses, becomes normative for the post-exilic restoration community.

2. The Poor and the Pious

What then of the followers of the prophets, with
their vision so different from that of the priests? Severe
problems seem to have arisen between these groups.
The prophetic group was convinced it was right and
that they were doing what God wanted, but they were
on the outs in the post-exilic community; they experienced misunderstanding and perhaps even persecution from their co-religionists. They are helpless to
do anything but put their trust completely in Yahweh
who will deliver them and vindicate them; they look
for the overthrow of their enemies.[2]

In the later additions to the book of Isaiah, the
Isaian Apocalypse (chs. 24–27) and Trito-Isaiah (chs.
56–66), we read passages such as these:

For you are a refuge to the poor,
a refuge to the needy in distress (25:4).

On that day, it will be said:
"Behold our God, to whom we looked to save us!
This is the Lord to whom we looked;
let us rejoice and be glad that he has saved us"
(25:9).

Trust in the Lord forever!
For the Lord is an eternal Rock.
He humbles those in high places,
and the lofty city he brings down.
He tumbles it to the ground,
levels it with the dust.
It is trampled underfoot by the needy,
by the footsteps of the poor.
The way of the just is smooth;
the path of the just you make level (26:4–7).

My watchmen are blind,
all of them unaware;
All of them are dumb dogs,
they cannot bark. . . .
These are the shepherds
who know no discretion;
Each of them goes his own way,
every one of them to his own gain. . . .

The just man perishes,
but no one takes it to heart;
Devout men are swept away,
with no one giving it a thought (56:10–57:1).

On high I dwell, and in holiness,
and with the crushed and dejected in spirit,

To revive the spirits of the dejected,
>to revive the hearts of the crushed (57:15).

This, rather, is the fasting that I wish:
>releasing those bound unjustly,
>untying the thongs of the yoke;
Setting free the oppressed,
>breaking every yoke;
Sharing your bread with the hungry,
>sheltering the oppressed and the homeless;
Clothing the naked when you see them,
>and not turning your back on your own
>>(58:6–7; cf. 58:9–10).

The spirit of the Lord God is upon me,
>because the Lord has anointed me;
He has sent me to bring glad tidings to the lowly,
>to heal the brokenhearted. . . .
You yourselves shall be named priests of the Lord
>(61:1, 6).

This is the one whom I approve:
>the lowly and afflicted man who trembles at my
>>word. . . .
Hear the word of the Lord
>you who tremble at his word:
Your brethren who, because of my name,
>hate and reject you, say,
"Let the Lord show his glory
>that we may see your joy";
>but they shall be put to shame (66:2, 5).

In these texts, we can see a growing frustration and sense of helplessness. Their brethren, co-religionists (66:5), who celebrate in the temple (58:1ff; 66:1) and keep fasts (58:3b–10), etc., hate them and reject them (66:5). But they, the afflicted and lowly who tremble at Yahweh's word (66:2, 5), are his servants (65:13) whom he approves (66:2). They eagerly await his coming to free them from oppression (61:1f) and put their enemies to shame (66:5). Then they, the servants of Yahweh (65:13), will become the true priests (61:6) of the Lord in place of the present "shepherds without discretion" (56:11).

Those who were oppressed and marginal in their society were convinced that they were approved by God, and they put all their trust in him and awaited his deliverance and vindication. It is precisely in this situation that terms like "poor' and "oppressed" (*'ani* and *'anawim*), which were primarily sociological terms, begin to take on special spiritual significance. These terms undergo a transition "from sociology to religion, from material poverty to poverty of soul."[3] The spirituality of the *'anawim* will now develop on its own.

3. The Poor in Spirit

Poverty of spirit, humility (*'anawah*), becomes a virtue of openness to God, of putting all one's trust in God. The term occurs in Zephaniah 2:3 (perhaps the earliest usage of the word in this sense) to describe the remnant which will survive the great "day of the Lord":

> Seek the Lord, all you humble of the earth
> who have observed his law;
> Seek justice, seek humility;
> perhaps you may be sheltered
> on the day of the Lord's anger.

It is especially in the Book of Psalms, though, that this theme is frequently expressed. Psalm 34 is a praise of God for having heard the prayer of the psalmist who now render thanks and praise. The psalmist is not only "afflicted" (*'ani*), but also one who fears the Lord (vv. 8, 10–11), takes refuge in him (vv. 9, 23), is just (vv. 18, 20), and is a servant of Yahweh (v. 23). Standing over against the psalmist is the evildoer (v. 17), the wicked and the enemies of the just (v. 22). The distinction is now less "rich and poor" but rather "poor and sinner." Psalm 37 presents a similar contrast between evildoers (vv. 1, 7, 9–10, 12) and the just who are also meek, afflicted and poor (vv. 11, 14) and put all their trust in Yahweh (vv. 3–7).

The theme of the poor who call on the Lord occurs particularly in psalms of lament, where the psalmist turns to God in distress and has confidence that the Lord will hear and deliver. It has been argued that these "poor" represent a distinct group, but this is doubtful.[4]

> To you I lift up my soul,
> 　　O Lord, my God.
> In you I trust, let me not be put to shame,
> 　　let not my enemies exult over me. . . .
> Good and upright is the Lord;
> 　　thus he shows sinners the way.
> He guides the humble to justice,
> 　　he teaches the humble his way. . . .
> Look toward me, and have pity on me,
> 　　for I am alone and afflicted (Ps 25:1, 9, 16).
>
> Happy the man who makes the Lord his trust;
> 　　who turns not to idolatry
> 　　or to those who stray after falsehood. . . .

But may all who seek you
    exult and be glad in you,
And may those who love your salvation
    say ever, "The Lord be glorified."
Though I am afflicted and poor
    yet the Lord thinks of me (Ps 40:5, 18).

Incline your ear, O Lord; answer me,
    for I am afflicted and poor.
Keep my life, for I am devoted to you
    (Ps 86:1–2).

See also 14:6; 18:28; 22:25, 27; 69:30, 33–34; 70:6; 74:19; 88:16; 102; 109:16, 22, 31. At the end of the Psalter, we find two references to the *'anawim* who are the Lord's people, the faithful, set over against sinners:

Great is our Lord and mighty in power;
    to his wisdom there is no limit.
The Lord sustains the lowly;
    the wicked he casts to the ground (Ps 147:5–6).

For the Lord loves his people,
    and he adorns the lowly with victory.
Let the faithful exult in glory (Ps 149:4–5).

We find a similar spirituality of the poor, of humility, expressed in the Book of Proverbs and in that of Ben Sira, both reflecting a more comfortable, upper-class background.

The curse of the Lord is on the house of the wicked,
    but the dwelling of the just he blesses.

> When he is dealing with the arrogant he is stern,
>> but to the humble he shows kindness
>>> (Pr 3:33–34).

> The fear of the Lord is training for wisdom,
>> and humility *('anawah)* goes before honors
>>> (Pr 15:33; cf. 18:12).

> The reward of humility and fear of the Lord
>> is riches, honor and life (Pr 22:4).

> My son, conduct your affairs with humility,
>> and you will be loved more than a giver of gifts.
> Humble yourself the more, the greater you are,
>> and you will find favor with God.
> For great is the power of God;
>> by the humble he is glorified (Sir 3:17–19).

See also Proverbs 16:19.

4. Conclusions

1. The time of the Babylonian exile was a period of great suffering, confusion and crisis for all the people of Israel. Various religious responses are found in the Old Testament. These differing responses and perspectives continued and were a source of tension in the restoration period as well, when the priests with the Torah emerged as the leaders of the community.

2. The conviction that God will relieve and redeem the poor and afflicted is expressed in a new key by the followers of the prophets, especially those of Isaiah. As a group they represented a vision in considerable tension with the official view of the priests; because of this they suffered oppression and even, perhaps, persecution. In this context, a connection was made between being actually oppressed and being pious and faithful. Since they have no hope or power of their own, they put all their trust in God to intervene and deliver them. From being sociological terms describing a negative condition, "poor" and "oppressed" (*'anawim*) begin to take on positive religious meaning.

3. From this beginning, the spirituality of the poor develops on its own, coming to expression particularly in the psalms, above all the psalms of lament. It also appears in some passages of the wisdom literature, which indicates that *'anawah,* humility, was not incompatible with a more comfortable situation.

7 THE COMMUNITY OF QUMRAN

Before turning to the New Testament, we should delay for a moment over some important evidence from the time of Jesus. In 1947, Arab shepherds discovered some scrolls in a cave, and the adventure of the Dead Sea Scrolls had begun.[1] Over the next several years, the hills of the Judean desert near the Dead Sea were scoured, hundreds of caves were searched, and additional manuscripts were discovered. Also, some ancient ruins, Kirbet Qumran, near the northwest end of the Dead Sea were excavated. It is now generally admitted that these ruins belonged to a religious group of ancient Judaism, a branch of the Essenes, who were responsible for many of the scrolls discovered. A survey of these sectarian documents shows several points relevant to the theme we are discussing.

The Qumraners knew, first of all, and reaffirmed that God is the defender of the poor and the oppressed. His mighty hand is with the poor (141);[2] he has redeemed the soul/life of the poor one (156, 165); he has not abandoned the fatherless or despised the poor, but has done marvels for the humble (*'anawim*) (166).

Further, they recognized that the "prince of the congregation," the Davidic Messiah, would establish God's kingdom forever, by judging the poor with righteousness and by dispensing justice for the oppressed of the land (208–209). Those members who did not live at Qumran but in "the towns and camps" were instructed to "place the earnings of at least two days out of every month into the hands of the Guardian and the Judges, and from it they shall give to the fatherless, and from it they shall succor the poor and the needy, the aged sick and the homeless, the captive taken by a foreign people. . . ." (116). They thus show their concern to alleviate poverty.

There is not, however, a great deal of talk along these lines, and the reason is not hard to find. The members of the sect were without real power. Regarding the Jerusalem priesthood and temple worship as corrupt, they had fled to the wilderness (86) where they experienced persecution from the "Wicked Priest" who had "betrayed the precepts for the sake of riches" (240). It is not surprising to see that they considered themselves to be among the poor and the oppressed. They considered as basic the spirit of humility (*'anawah*) (e.g., 75, 76, 78), and they themselves were *'anawim* (166); the phrase, "poor-humble of spirit" occurs (142). In the Hymns, the writer often refers to himself as the "poor one" whom God protects (e.g., 156, 159, 165, 166). The term, "the Poor" (*'ebyonim*) seems at times to be almost a title of the group itself (the "congregation of the Poor," 244, 245), though scholars dispute this.[3]

The group is also very much aware of the danger of riches. In fact, this theme recurs rather frequently. They must not desire "violent riches" (91); men of injustice are those who are zealous for wealth (92); riches are one of Satan's three nets to ensnare Israel (101); they are warned to keep away from the "unclean riches of wickedness acquired by vow or anathema from

the temple treasury; they shall not rob the poor of
his people, to make of widows their prey and of the
fatherless their victim" (103). Sinners act arrogantly
(i.e., are not "humble") for the sake of riches and
gain (105). Riches are connected with pride, arrogance
and injustice, and no riches can be compared with
God's truth (196). The crisis in Jerusalem, against which
the Qumraners were reacting, was closely connected
to the buying and selling of the high-priestly office
and the subsequent injustice and extravagance of the
Hasmonean "priest-kings." They knew from experience
how the desire for riches led to forsaking God's law.[4]

The Essenes living at Qumran went even further.
They held their goods in common; they shared their
possessions. After a period of probation, during which
his money was set aside but not mingled with that
of the group, the candidate was received to full mem-
bership. At this time his earnings and possessions were
handed over to the steward to be joined to the possessions of the community (82, 72, 78). If he held
back anything or lied, a punishment was attached (82).

The motivation for this is not entirely clear. Surely
they were reacting against the dangers of riches noted
above. But more positively, they wished to form a true
community, an intimate fellowship (78) in which they
already began to live the life of the new age, an age
in which the disparity between rich and poor, wicked
and oppressed would be gone.[5]

Archeological finds have some bearing on this. No
coins have been found in the caves where individuals
lived. Only the community center at Qumran has yield-
ed coins. Here an intriguing discovery was a cache
of over five hundred and fifty coins found in the work-
room area. Several explanations have been proposed.

Was it someone hiding his money and holding out on the community? Was it an embezzling overseer? Was it an old overseer who had died without telling where the community pot was stashed? We will never know for certain.[6]

The life and thought of the Qumran community reflect then several Old Testament themes we have detected so far:

1. God is the defender of the poor; his prince will be likewise.

2. The Qumraners must use their money to alleviate and end poverty, either by setting aside money to be given to the poor or by their common sharing.

3. While not being economically poor, they are members of the "poor" and the "oppressed" who depend entirely on God and look solely to him for their ultimate deliverance.

4. The danger of riches in leading to arrogance, a haughty heart, and injustice is clearly recognized.

None of these are irrelevant to the New Testament, to which we now turn.

8 JESUS

We now come to the New Testament. Here we will be dealing largely, but not exclusively, with the synoptic gospels and the Acts of the Apostles. First, Jesus, his life and teaching, will be examined, and then the way this is reflected in the life and teaching of the early Christian community.

1. His Life

Theologians tell us that when we speak of beginnings and endings, protology and eschatology, birth and death, whether individual or cosmic, we cannot use our normal, everyday, descriptive language. As important as these events are for us, none of us has direct experience of them that we can speak about. Thus we talk of them only in a language which is indirect, highly symbolic and even "mythic" in a technical sense of the word. This general principle must be kept in mind as we approach the New Testament statements about the birth and death of Jesus.[1]

These two moments are discussed, we find, in terms of poverty. Jesus is born in a stable; on the occasion of Mary's purification and the consecration of the child, his parents did not have a lamb to offer, so they made the offering of the poor, two turtle doves (Lk 2:7, 22–24). In describing the meaning of Jesus' incarnation, Paul reminds the Corinthians "how for your sake he made himself poor though he was rich, so that you might become rich by his poverty" (2 Cor 8:9); he likewise exhorts the Philippians to be humble in imitation of Jesus who "emptied himself and took the form of a slave . . . obediently accepting even death, death on a cross . . . so that at Jesus' name every knee must bend . . . and every tongue proclaim . . . that Jesus Christ is Lord" (Phil 2:6–11).[2] Jesus' whole life and work is put under the sign of poverty, of a radical self-emptying in order to do the will of the Father who sent him.

When it comes to details of Jesus' life on earth, of what happened in between his birth and death, we are at a bit of a disadvantage because the New Testament sources do not give us the precise kind of information we would like. We are generally aware of the problems involved in the so-called "search for the historical Jesus." While an earlier generation of scholars were more skeptical in this regard, scholars today feel that we can attain certain broad characteristics of Jesus' life and teaching.

To the best of our knowledge, most of Jesus' life, over thirty years, was spent in Nazareth where he grew up with his family, learning the trade of Joseph, the carpenter (Mk 6:3; Mt 13:55), working with his hands. Jesus and his family belonged to the broad social class of the poor, of those who had to work for their living.

In his public life, Jesus lived as an itinerant preacher[3] who "had nowhere to lay his head" (Mt 8:20; Lk 9:58) and who was not anxious about what he would eat, drink or wear (Mt 6:26–34); he devoted himself to the preaching of the kingdom. As he traveled through Palestine, he was accompanied by a group of disciples which included many women who helped minister to his needs (Lk 8:1–3; 23:49). The group had a common purse (or money box—Jn 12:6; 13:29)[4] to provide for their needs, as well as to have something to give to the poor. "There is no reason to think that Jesus deliberately impoverished himself in order to lead a mendicant life, or that he was unusually poor by contemporary standards."[5]

Jesus had wealthy friends—Nicodemus (Jn 3:1–21; 7:50; 19:39); Joseph of Arimathea (Mk 15:43–46; Mt 27:57–60; Lk 23:50–54; Jn 19:38–42); Zacchaeus (Lk 19:1–10)—and he does not hesitate to visit them and to dine with them (e.g., Lk 19:1–10; 7:36; 14:1). While he is at dinner at one of their houses, a certain woman anoints him with precious oil which, we are told, could have been sold and the proceeds given to the poor; he rebukes his critics and approves the woman's actions (Mk 14:3–9; Jn 12:1–8). In comparison with John the Baptist, Jesus is reproached for eating and drinking with and for being a friend of toll-gatherers and sinners (Mk 2:16; Lk 5:30–31; 7:34; 19:7; Mt 9:11; 11:19).

We can see from this brief survey that Jesus' attitude to material things was one of complete freedom. They were not for him a source of anxiety or preoccupation. He could use and enjoy them or not as the occasion demanded. Attempts to present Jesus as a dirty, destitute beggar at any time of his life are completely without biblical foundation.[6] His first concern was to preach the gospel of the kingdom, and it is to this that we now turn our attention.

2. His Teaching.[7]

The first striking characteristic of Jesus' preaching of the kingdom is that it appears particularly as good news to the poor. Luke presents Jesus at the start of his ministry in the synagogue of Nazareth where he reads from Isaiah 61:1–2a:

> He has sent me to bring glad tidings to the poor,
>   to proclaim liberty to captives,
> Recovery of sight to the blind
>   and release to prisoners,
> To announce a year of favor from the Lord.

Then he proclaims, "Today this Scripture passage is fulfilled in your hearing" (Lk 4:14–22).

John the Baptist sent some of his disciples to Jesus to ask, "Are you he who is to come?" Jesus replied:

> Go back and report to John what you hear and see: the blind recover their sight, cripples walk, lepers are cured, the deaf hear, dead men are raised to life, and the poor have the good news preached to them (Mt 11:5; Lk 7:22).

Then the beatitudes, in what is most likely their more original form, announced:

> Blessed are the poor, for the kingdom of God is
>   theirs.
> Blessed are the afflicted, for they shall be consoled.
> Blessed are the hungry, for they shall be filled
>   (cf. Mt 5:3, 6; Lk 6:20–21).

Jesus' mission and teaching is one of preaching the kingdom of God which is seen as a manifestation of God's mercy and consolation and justice directed especially to the poor, the hungry and the oppressed.

Who are these special beneficiaries of the kingdom, the "poor," and why are they so blessed? Exegetes and spiritual writers have commonly answered this question by seeing in these people the New Testament continuation of the Old Testament *'anawim.* According to this common opinion, the "poor" who are the beneficiaries of Jesus' preaching are not a particular social or economic class, people suffering from actual physical want, but a religious group whose spiritual dispositions open them in a special way to hear and receive the proclamation of the kingdom.[8]

The New Testament does not allow us to accept this opinion as an answer to our question. While we may possibly spiritualize poverty in this way, what of the persecuted, the lepers, the blind, the dead, cripples—to all of whom Jesus' coming is good news? For all of these, the gospel means precisely that their state of affliction is at an end: "the blind see, the deaf hear, lepers are cured, etc." In these texts, the poor must be those who in fact suffer from economic need and social oppression.[9]

But why are they blessed? The basis for this does not lie, as we have seen, in the attitude of the "poor" toward God. It is to be found rather in the attitude of God to the poor. To understand this, we need to recall what we saw above about the ancient Near Eastern idea of the king whose basic function was to guarantee justice in the realm, especially for those most exposed to injustice. The condition of poverty is an evil, a scandal, an affront to the royal justice of God who, through his Messiah, has decided to put an end to it. In his preaching, Jesus affirms that this kingdom has now come, and this is good news particularly for the poor and the oppressed. They are blessed, not because of their spiritual dispositions, but because God wishes to make his kingdom a shining manifestation of his love and justice.

If the coming of the kingdom is good news especially for the poor, what about everyone else, all the other people? They are by no means excluded; the gospel is proclaimed to all humanity. We noted above that Jesus was criticized for eating and drinking with the wealthy. In replying to his critics he says, "People who are in good health do not need a doctor; sick people do" (Mt 9:12; Lk 5:31; Mk 2:17). Jesus preaches not only to the physically poor and sick (many of whom he healed), but also to those who are sick and poor in other ways and who turn to God in their distress.

The parable of the publican and the Pharisee makes this point with great clarity (Lk 18:9–14). To appreciate this we must acquaint ourselves with the social conditions at Jesus' time. The Pharisees were a group, primarily of lay people, who were not conspicuous for being either wealthy or powerful, though some individuals may have been. The Sadducees, on the other hand, were quite willing to cooperate with the ruling Roman power and so held the high offices of prestige and influence. The Pharisees (whose name probably means "Separatist") held themselves apart from this kind of cooperation, basing their claim to respect and authority solely on their religious integrity, their fidelity to the Law. The toll-gatherers (a better translation than publican or tax-collector, as a recent study has shown[10]) were engaged in collecting tolls for the government; their own profit came from what they collected over and above what the government had demanded. They became wealthy by extorting from others more than was just (see, for example, Lk 3:12). The hearers of Jesus would have expected the faithful, pious, religious leader to be praised and the wealthy oppressor to be rebuked. The conclusion of the parable is well known: the toll-gatherer goes home justified.[11] Why? Because he recognized his own sinfulness and need and turned to God in humble admission of the fact. He had begun to empty himself before God, while the Pharisee, through his self-righteousness, was closed in on himself. The toll-gatherer thus expressed and truly shared in the spirituality of the 'anawim, which we discussed above.

Both of these aspects of Jesus' teaching, his call to put an end to suffering and poverty, and his preaching to all who open themselves in faith, appear in the episode of the toll-gatherer, Zacchaeus (Lk 19:1–10). Jesus responds to Zacchaeus' eagerness and openness to hear the gospel; he goes and dines with him. Resisting the murmurings of the self-righteous crowd, Zacchaeus "stood his ground and said to the Lord: 'I give half of my belongings, Lord, to the poor. If I have defrauded anyone in the least, I pay him back fourfold.' " Jesus preaches the kingdom to all, calling them to be converted, to do penance, to open themselves to receive God, recognizing their need and dependency on him. They must become 'anawim. They in turn are called to join in and continue Jesus' royal work of bringing good news to the poor, of putting an end to poverty, hunger and injustice. God's eschatological kingdom is a new kind of society. Oppression is as much an affliction of the oppressor as it is a problem for the oppressed. The example of Zacchaeus is very instructive in this regard.

9 THE EARLY CHRISTIAN COMMUNITY

In addition to testimony regarding the life and teaching of Jesus, the New Testament contains evidence also of the way that the early Church, the immediate followers of Jesus, received and lived his gospel. In regard to the question of poverty, we want to look at four aspects of the life and teaching of the early Church: (1) the primitive community in the Acts of the Apostles; (2) the writings of Paul; (3) the demand to see one's possessions in the context of the call to discipleship; (4) Matthew's version of the beatitudes.

1. Acts: No One Was in Need[1]

In the Acts of the Apostles, Luke presents several summaries which describe the life of the early Jerusalem community. The first appears in 2:42-47 and includes the notice that "those who believed shared all things in common; they would sell their property and goods, dividing everything on the basis of each one's need." It is only in the second summary (4:32-35) that we find this theme developed more fully:

The community of believers were of one heart and one mind. None of them ever claimed anything as his own; rather everything was held in common.

66

With power the apostles bore witness to the resurrection of the Lord Jesus, and great respect was paid to them all; nor was anyone needy among them, for all who owned property or houses sold them and donated the proceeds. They used to lay them at the feet of the apostles to be distributed to everyone according to his need.

A broad consensus exists among scholars that Luke is less interested in presenting an accurate historical description of the early Christian community and more concerned to present the Christians of his church with an ideal of Christian life.[2] The two incidents which follow (Barnabas and Ananias and Sapphira) suggest that the ideal described by Luke was not always realized. Further, it is expressly affirmed (5:4) that Ananias was not obliged to sell his property or, having sold it, to give the proceeds to the apostles.

If, as seems clear, Luke is presenting an ideal, what exactly is it? Luke writes, "Those who believed shared all things in common" (2:44); "everything was held in common" (4:32); the "community of believers was of one heart and mind" (4:32). Reading these things, Luke's Greek readers could not help but recall several well-known Greek proverbs: "Among friends, everything is in common" (not unlike the English, "What's mine is yours"); "Friends have nothing of their own"; and for the Greeks, friendship consisted precisely in being one heart and mind, one soul. Luke then is presenting his readers with an ideal whose Greek name is friendship, but whose Christian name is *agape,* love.[3] It is not an ideal of poverty. The first summary in 2:42–47 encircles the reference to shared goods with the deeper reality of shared faith, worship and prayer.

The Christian community, through its sharing and caring, is called not to be poor in the sense of material destitution, but to continue Christ's work of putting an end to poverty so that no one will be in need.

2. The Writings of Paul

When we come to the Pauline writings, we discover that the terms "rich" and "poor" scarcely occur.[4] Whether we can conclude from this that Paul's communities were predominately "upper class" is open to dispute.[5] Be that as it may, we can conclude fairly safely that the question of economic poverty does not seem to have been a pressing one. Several points can, however, be made in regard to our theme.

Paul stresses the need to work. While preaching the gospel for free (1 Cor 9:1–18), he worked to support himself and his needs (Acts 18:3; 20:34; 2 Thes 3:8–10) and demanded that Christians likewise work to provide for their needs. Even the expectation of the *parousia,* the second coming of Christ, did not dispense from this obligation (1 Thes 4:12; 2 Thes 3:8–10).

Paul also stresses the obligation of Christians to care for others when they are in need. This is, in fact, a common theme in the early Church (e.g., Eph 4:28; 1 Tim 6:17–19; Jas 1:27; 2:14–17; 1 Jn 3:17). He himself had been the beneficiary of such care more than once (e.g., Phil 2:25–29; 4:10–20). Citing the example of Christ becoming human to save us, Paul reminds the Corinthians that they cannot separate spiritual and physical concerns. If they truly live in Christ, they cannot turn their backs on brothers and sisters in need (a lesson similar to that of Mt 25:31–46):[6]

I am not giving an order but simply testing your generous love against the concern which others show. You are well acquainted with the favor shown you by our Lord Jesus Christ; how for your sake he made himself poor though he was rich, so that you might become rich by his poverty. I am about to give you some advice on this matter of rich and poor. It will help you who began this good work last year, not only to carry it through, but to do so willingly.... The willingness to give should accord with one's means, not go beyond them. The relief of others ought not to impoverish you; there should be a certain equality. Your plenty at the present time should supply their need, so that their surplus may one day supply your need, with equality as the result (2 Cor 8:8–15).

In regard to possessions, Paul urges a certain independence, an interior detachment, so that having or not having things will not disturb him. "Whatever the situation I find myself in, I have learned to be self-sufficient (*autarkes*)" (Phil 4:11). *Autarkeia*, "self-sufficiency," was an important and prominent virtue among the Stoic philosophers of Paul's time, and he was certainly influenced by this fact. The same theme recurs in the later epistles (e.g., 1 Tim 6:6–9). For Paul, though, it was not the result of personal struggle and achievement. It was the gift of the risen Christ: "In him who is the source of my strength, I have strength for everything" (Phil 4:13). It is striking that in this context we do not find an appeal to the theme of the *'anawim*.[7]

3. Come, Follow Me

A feature recurring in several (but not all) of the
calls to discipleship is the demand to "sell all one's
possessions and give to the poor." These texts have
often been appealed to in discussions of Christian poverty. We will concern ourselves here with two texts:
the call of the rich man, and the Lukan "catechism
of discipleship."

The story of the call of the rich man is a familiar
one (Mk 10:17–22; Lk 18:18–23; Mt 19:16–22).[8] A man
approaches Jesus and asks what means he should take
to receive a share in eternal life. Jesus recalls the commandments of the Law. "All these things," he replies,
"I have kept from my childhood." Jesus, looking on
him with love, continues, "There is one more thing
you must do. Go and sell what you have and give
it to the poor; you will then have treasure in heaven.
After that, come and follow me." But the man went
away, "for he had many possessions."

This scene appears in each of the synoptic gospels,
each time with certain redactional variations. We cannot
study these in detail here but will summarize the conclusions of scholars on this passage. The New Testament continually recognizes that riches and
possessions represent one of the greatest obstacles to
true faith in God (e.g., Mt 6:19–21). Things in themselves are not bad; it is rather that they so easily become
idols. We anchor our faith, our security and our identity
in them and not in God. The young man who was
very wealthy was called by Jesus to put his faith where
it belongs. How can one truly follow Jesus without
sharing this *'anawim* faith? But for this particular person, riches indeed were an obstacle. The episode of
the rich man is essentially a story about the true nature

of faith. If one's possessions become an obstacle, a choice must be faced; do we serve God or mammon (Mt 6:24; Lk 16:13)?

This demand is not addressed only to that particular rich man, nor is it restricted to a select group within the Christian community. It concerns all Christians; the demands of faith are the same for all. The means proposed to the rich man are imposed on all Christians each time that the call to grow in the Christian life demands it. J. Murphy-O'Connor draws this conclusion: "The believer must be free of wealth in the sense that possessions must not limit his perspectives, but he is obliged to put them aside only if and when they constitute an obstacle to faith."[9]

We find a similar teaching in Luke's "catechism of discipleship" (14:25–33).[10] Like Matthew, he is addressing a community already Christian, already dedicated to the following of Christ. As the parables of the man building the tower and of the king going to war indicate, Christians are being warned to follow through on their commitment lest they become a laughing-stock. Two of the most persistent and difficult obstacles to this are family and possessions. If and when the family becomes an obstacle, the Christian must choose. If and when possessions become an obstacle, the Christian must choose. Neither family nor possessions must become such an obstacle, but they may; and when this happens, the Christian must take a stand. Where is his or her faith?

4. The Poor in Spirit

"Blessed are the poor." This beatitude, as preserved by Luke in its more original form, dealt with the materially poor and disadvantaged. The coming of God's kingdom signified that their poverty was at an end. In focusing on this, Luke was challenging his readers to continue Jesus' work of bringing in God's kingdom, of putting an end to poverty and injustice through their mutual love and concern and their sharing of goods so that no one be in need.[11]

When we come to Matthew, we are on a completely different level. In his version of the beatitudes, he speaks of the "poor in spirit" and of those who "hunger and thirst for justice (Mt 5:3, 6). Matthew presents his Sermon on the Mount as a new "Law" for Christians, setting before them the spiritual values and dispositions characteristic of those living in the kingdom. He expressly picks up the theme of the *'anawim*, the humble ones who place all their faith in God and depend on him alone. Poverty in a material sense is an evil which the Messiah has come to terminate. In order to make "poverty" a Christian virtue, to give it positive content, Matthew speaks of "poverty of spirit," i.e., meekness and humility in imitation of Jesus who was "meek and humble of heart" (Mt 11:29). "The phrase refers to those whose spirit is impoverished, downtrodden by circumstances. . . . In his own way, Matthew has preserved the note of eschatological reversal, and has prevented a strictly economic interpretation of the beatitudes as well."[12] Here again we are dealing with the nature of Christian faith.

10 GOSPEL POVERTY: WITNESS TO THE RISEN CHRIST

In our first chapter, we discussed the kinds of guidelines for our lives we might expect to find in the Scriptures, and there we noted two: negative and positive. As we conclude our survey of the biblical data on poverty, this is, in fact, what we find.

I. NEGATIVE CONCLUSIONS

1. Poverty Is an Evil. On the negative side, we see that poverty in the sense of economic deprivation, of lacking the necessities of life, is never a biblical virtue. It is a scandal, the result of sin, and an affront to the royal justice of God. Nowhere in the Bible do we find any indication that destitution can be a good. The poor cry out to Yahweh to deliver them (e.g., Ex 2:23–25); poverty leads to breaking God's law (e.g. Pr 30:7–9). It is an evil which the Messiah, ushering in God's kingdom, puts to an end.

If poverty in a real economic sense were to be a biblical ideal, then so would be blindness, lameness, deafness, leprosy, etc., for these are all listed together (e.g., Mt 11:4–5; Lk 7:22) as evils terminated by the work of the Messiah. The good news is precisely that

the blind see, the deaf hear, the lame walk, etc. And
the poor have the good news preached to them, the
good news that their poverty is over.

The biblical assessment of poverty as an evil has
been well phrased by G. Gutierrez in his *A Theology
of Liberation*:

> If *material poverty* is something to be rejected, as
> the Bible vigorously insists, then a witness of pov-
> erty cannot make of it a Christian ideal. This would
> be to aspire to a condition which is recognized
> as degrading to man. It would be, moreover, to
> move against the current of history. It would be
> to oppose any idea of the domination of nature
> by man and the consequent and progressive cre-
> ation of better conditions of life. And finally, but
> not least seriously, it would be to justify, even if
> involuntarily, the injustice and exploitation which
> is the cause of poverty.[1]

In the history of Christianity we do note various
movements which have tried to make a virtue of material deprivation. Material things are considered bad;
they cannot but corrupt the purity and integrity of
their owners. In order to keep ourselves undefiled, we
must remove ourselves as far as possible from material
things. Underlying this attitude is a deeper theological
issue: a radical distrust of creation.[2] The recurrence
of this attitude in such forms as Gnosticism, Manichaeism, Albigensianism, Jansenism, etc., testifies to its
tenacity and appeal. Scripture emphatically affirms both

the goodness of the world and humanity's radical root-edness in the world. The problem with material things is not that they are bad and must be avoided, but that they are good and too many people do not have enough because others have too much. The Christian corrective to misuse of material things is not no use but proper use.

2. Riches Are a Danger. At the other extreme, the biblical tradition recognizes that riches represent a great danger to our life with God. They can make us proud and arrogant, and almost always involve sin, injustice and oppression (e.g., Pr 30:7–9; Sir 31:1–11; Am 8:4–6; Isa 1:23–27; 10:1–4, etc.). The danger of riches in the following of Christ is a recurrent theme in the gospels (e.g., Mt 6:19–34; Lk 12:33–34; 16:13–15; 1 Tim 6:8–10; James 5:1–6). And riches are dangerous because they so easily become idols; we worship the great god, Mammon.

In the history of the Church, we also note various attempts to root the possession of great wealth in a theological position. Working hard, saving money, and being rich are signs of being just, a sign of God's blessing and election. Being poor, on the other hand, is a sign of being lazy and sinful. Even though some Old Testament texts can be found that lean in this direction, the Old Testament itself admits much greater complexity, as the Book of Job so eloquently attests. This kind of idea creeps all too easily into various kinds of predestinationism, e.g. Calvinism and Puritanism, and some forms of capitalism.

Both material poverty and material riches are negatively evaluated in the biblical tradition. Neither extreme can be romanticized and presented as virtuous or as an ideal. Each needs the positive witness of biblical poverty.

II. POSITIVE CONCLUSIONS

1. Radical Faith. We have discussed what biblical poverty is not; we now have to consider its positive side. Here the biblical evidence points to two distinct but related areas. The first of these is radical faith in God. In the Old Testament, for all the periods we have examined, the first and most basic demand of the covenant—either Mosaic or Davidic—is faith in God. In the later exilic and post-exilic period, this faith begins to be spoken of in terms of *'anawah,* humility, meekness. Developing the Old Testament theme of the *'anawim,* the "poor in spirit" of the New Testament recognize their dependence on God and place their whole lives under his care. Mary, the mother of the Lord, is presented as a model of this kind of faith (Lk 1:46–55).[3] Material things (also one's family is mentioned) present the strongest and most common distraction and obstacle to this kind of faith. Christians must be ready to sacrifice their possessions, or anything else for that matter, if and when these become obstacles to their growth in faith. This is the basic teaching of the gospel story of the call of the rich man, of the Lukan catechism of discipleship, and of Matthew's version of the beatitudes.

This idea is often expressed in terms of detachment. We must detach ourselves from those things which too easily lead us astray. But this is to phrase it only from a negative point of view. Positively, the faith aspect of gospel poverty demands a radical rooting of ourselves and our lives in God, a positive attachment to him. We recognize that our whole lives, as well as all of creation, are gift, and we stand open before the Father, receiving his gift, acknowledging and thanking him for it. Gutierrez again has expressed this well:

Our analysis of the biblical texts concerning *spiritual poverty* has helped us to see that it is not directly or in the first instance an interior detachment from the goods of this world, a spiritual attitude which becomes authentic by incarnating itself in material poverty. Spiritual poverty is something more complete and profound. It is above all total availability to the Lord. Its relationship to the use or ownership of economic goods is inescapable but secondary and partial. Spiritual childhood— an ability to receive, not a passive acceptance— defines the total posture of human existence before God, men and things.[4]

2. Outpouring Charity. The second positive area to which the biblical data point is charity, a charity which includes as an integral part of itself an active concern to put an end to poverty, hunger, injustice and oppression. This is not a private virtue but affects the structure of society and of natural creation as well. Yahweh delivered the Israelites from the oppression of Egypt; they in turn, living out the covenant, were not to oppress others. As king of Israel, Yahweh was concerned for the establishing of justice in the realm and for defending the weak and helpless. The king and the wealthy were called to use their power to bring about a kingdom where God's justice and mercy would be manifest. As God's Messiah, Jesus preached the advent of God's kingdom, a kingdom bringing with it a radical reversal of the status quo. As part of this, Jesus preached the good news that poverty was at an end; the Christian community continues his work in caring for each other and sharing what they have so that no one will suffer basic need. It is not that everyone has the same, but that each one's basic needs are cared for.[5]

In the parable of the sheep and the goats (Mt 25:31–46), Jesus sets before us the basis for salvation and damnation at the last judgment. "I was hungry and you gave me to eat; thirsty, and you gave me to drink, etc." It is significant that Jesus did not say in reproach, "I was hungry and you did not become hungry with me; thirsty, and you did not become thirsty with me, etc." That would not be putting an end to these conditions. The Christian is called to continue Christ's work of bringing in God's kingdom of peace, love and justice. We say very casually in the Our Father, "Thy kingdom come," without always realizing how deeply our lives could change if we were to take seriously the implications of that phrase.

As we saw above, the attempt to make material need and abundant riches into virtues is often rooted in deeper theological positions. In considering these two aspects of the Bible's positive teaching on poverty, we can also go a step deeper. In saying that biblical poverty means faith and charity, we are speaking ultimately of our sharing, through Jesus, in the Trinitarian life. What does it mean to say that Jesus is the Son, the second person of the Trinity? It means, at least, two things. On the one hand, it tells us that his whole existence is received. The Father pours out everything of himself except his being Father, and the Son receives it. On the other hand, the Son gives it all back. He returns everything except his being Son, in love to the Father. This bond of loving return is the Spirit. Being Son then means a complete openness to receive all from the Father and a complete return of everything to the Father in the Spirit of love.

When the Son became incarnate, both of these aspects are reflected. Paul says, "Being rich, he became poor," and "He emptied himself." This complete openness to God, to receive all from him, is expressed in the image of Jesus' nakedness in the crib and on the cross. Jesus himself is the first of the *'anawim.* But we cannot stop there. He empties himself, true, but only to be filled with the Father's will, "so that you might become rich by his poverty." The life and teaching of Jesus manifest the Father's will to reconcile all of creation and the whole human race to himself in the Spirit of love. Jesus has poured out his Spirit on us to bring us to share in the inner life of the Trinity, to carry us back to the fullness of life in God.

This double aspect emerges also in Jesus' teaching. He demands the openness of faith, the recognition that everything is gift, the spirit of the *'anawim.* The other side of this is the call to discipleship, to share in the spreading of the kingdom of love and justice. True to his teaching, the early Christian community also reflects these aspects with its stress on the radical nature of true faith and on the obligation of the community to work to put an end to poverty, oppression and injustice of every kind, so that "no one be in need."

3. A Definition. We are now in a position to offer a definition of biblical poverty. It is not defined in relation to an economic or a social condition, nor in relation to material things. These change too much and too quickly. It is defined in relation to God. Biblical poverty is the manner in which our living of the Trinitarian life, opened to us in and through Jesus, bears consequences in our relation to material things. If we truly put our faith in God and root our dependency in him, we will not seek to base our identity, our security, our faith in material possessions. We will not be driven to acquire more and more, beyond our basic and truly human needs. And if we truly live the life of charity, working to bring in the kingdom of justice and love, this will manifest itself in the way we use what we have. Am I truly concerned about injustice, hunger, oppression? The Christian by his or her life does not witness *to* poverty. All through the Scriptures, poverty is an evil. The Christian witnesses to the presence of the risen Lord in our midst, guiding us, strengthening us, calling us to share ever more deeply in his own Trinitarian life of love. This cannot but affect the way we live with, think about and use material things.

SELECTED BIBLIOGRAPHY

B. C. Birch and L. L. Rasmussen, *The Predicament of the Prosperous (Biblical Perspectives on Current Issues)* (Philadelphia: Westminster Press, 1978).

A. Gelin, *The Poor of Yahweh* (Collegeville: The Liturgical Press, 1964).

Gospel Poverty: Essays in Biblical Theology (Chicago: Franciscan Herald Press, 1977). The five essays in this important collection are the following:

A. George, "Poverty in the Old Testament," 3–24.

J. Dupont, "The Poor and Poverty in the Gospels and Acts," 25–52.

S. Légasse, "The Call of the Rich Man," 53–80.

P. Seidensticker, "St. Paul and Poverty," 81–120.

B. Rigaux, "The Radicalism of the Kingdom," 121–150.

M. Hengel, *Property and Riches in the Early Church* (Philadelphia: Fortress Press, 1974).

R. J. Karris, *What Are They Saying About Luke-Acts?* (New York: Paulist Press, 1979).

J. B. Metz, *Poverty of Spirit* (New York: Paulist Press, 1968).

P. F. Mulhern, *Dedicated Poverty, Its History and Theology* (Staten Island: Alba House, 1973).

J. Murphy-O'Connor, *What Is Religious Life? A Critical Reappraisal* (Wilmington, Del.: Michael Glazier, 1977).

T. Roszak, *Person/Planet* (Garden City, N.Y.: Doubleday, 1978).

The Way: Supplement No. 9 (Spring 1970). The entire issue is devoted to "Poverty."

NOTES

Abbreviations

ANET   *Ancient Near Eastern Texts Relating to the Old Testament* (J.B. Pritchard, ed.; Princeton, N.J.: University Press, 1966)

CBQ   *Catholic Biblical Quarterly*

GP   *Gospel Poverty.* See Bibliography.

IDB   *Interpreter's Dictionary of the Bible.*

IDBS   *Interpreter's Dictionary of the Bible, Supplement Volume.*

Int   *Interpretation.*

JBC   *Jerome Biblical Commentary* (Englewood Cliffs, N.J.: Prentice-Hall, 1967).

JBL   *Journal of Biblical Literature.*

JNES   *Journal of Near Eastern Studies.*

NCE   *New Catholic Encyclopedia.*

NRT   *Nouvelle revue théologique.*

NTS   *New Testament Studies.*

TDOT   *Theological Dictionary of the Old Testament* (Grand Rapids, Mich.: W. Eerdmans)

1 Background Ideas

1. "In the New Testament what distinguishes the 'rich' from other social classes is the fact that they are not bound to labor; they can make captial work

for them": J. Murphy-O'Connor, *What Is Religious Life?* 46. See also P. Seidensticker, *GP*, 81–82. While it might offend our American egalitarianism, I suspect that this distinction is not as irrelevant today as we might think. "America's dirty little secret is not sex. It is not power. Nor is it success. America's dirty little secret is class. It remains a secret even to some of its most cruelly treated victims": R. McAfee Brown, quoting J. Anthony Lukas, *Christian Century* 96 #1 (Jan. 3–10, 1979), 6.

2. The role of the Bible in Christian moral theology is a rather complex question. For a fine introduction, including a survey of recent opinion, see B. C. Birch and L. L. Rasmussen, *Bible and Ethics in the Christian Life* (Minneapolis: Augsburg Pub. House, 1976). More narrowly, see C. Curran, *Contemporary Problems in Moral Theology* (Notre Dame: Fides Press, 1970) 233–239; *Catholic Moral Theology in Dialogue* (Notre Dame: Fides Press, 1972) 24–64. On Jesus' teachings as goal commands, see C. Curran, *A New Look at Christian Morality* (Notre Dame: Fides Press, 1968) 1–23, now reprinted in *Themes in Fundamental Moral Theology* (Notre Dame: University Press, 1977) 5–26.

3. A. George, *GP*, 4–6. On the uses of the New Testament words for "poor," see J. Dupont, *GP*, 26–27.

2 The Bible and the World

1. This theme could, of course, be developed at much greater length. For indications of the questions involved, see B. C. Birch and L. L. Rasmussen, *Predicament*, 112–125; H. W. Wolff, *Anthropology of the Old Testament* (Philadelphia: Fortress, 1974); W. Zimmerli, *The Old Testament and the World* (Atlanta: John Knox

Press, 1976). At times the New Testament uses "world" in a negative sense, but this is when the world is seen as the sphere of sin and has nothing to do with being material as such. See C. R. North, "World, the," *IDB* 4, 877–878. Without noting it, Theodore Roszak, *Person/Planet* (Garden City, N.Y.: Doubleday, 1978) reflects the biblical world-view through and through.

3 Exodus and Sinai

1. For fuller discussion of questions relating to the exodus and Sinai, one can consult R. de Vaux, *The Early History of Israel* (Philadelphia: Westminster Press, 1978) 320–472; J. Bright, *A History of Israel* (2nd ed.; Philadelphia: Westminster Press, 1972) 105–130.

2. Many scholars understand the Sinai covenant in the light of ancient Near Eastern treaties. I follow those scholars who disagree and see the Sinai covenant as expressing primarily kinship. See D. McCarthy, *Treaty and Covenant* (2nd ed.; Rome: Biblical Institute Press, 1978) 254–255, 268–269, 274; R. Sklba, "The Redeemer of Israel," *CBQ* 34 (1972) 1–18. While the term *"go'el"* does not occur explicitly in Exodus 19–24, it seems a valid inference. See again, R. Sklba, "Redeemer," 13–17. On *go'el,* see H. Ringgren; "ga'al," *TDOT* 2, 350–355. On the obligation to help the poor and defenseless, see F. C. Fensham, "Widow, Orphan and the Poor in Ancient Near Eastern Legal and Wisdom Literature," *JNES* 21 (1962) 129–139. I drew on these also for my discussion in *Covenant in the Old Testament* (*Herald Biblical Booklets;* Chicago: Franciscan Herald Press, 1975) 20–21.

4 Royal Theology and the Words of the Wise

1. On royal theology see S. Szikszai, "King, Kingship," *IDB* 3, 11–17; D. McCarthy, *Kings and Prophets* (Milwaukee: Bruce, 1968) 52–65; W. Brueggemann, "Kingship and Chaos," *CBQ* 33 (1971) 317–332. Perhaps the best short summary of Canaanite and Israelite royal theology is W. L. Humphreys, *Crisis and Story* (Palo Alto: Mayfield Publishing Co., 1979) 57–64.

2. W. Brueggemann, "Kingship and Chaos," 318–322.

3. H. H. Schmidt, *Gerechtigkeit als Weltordnung. Hintergrund und Geschichte der alttestamentlichen Gerechtigkeitsbegriffes* (Tübingen: Mohr, 1968).

4. *ANET*, 164, 178.

5. M. D. Coogan, *Stories of Ancient Canaan* (Philadelphia: Westminster Press, 1978) 73–74.

6. W. Brueggemann, "Yahwist," *IDBS*, 971–975; W. L. Humphreys, *Crisis*, 65–78; H. W. Wolff, "The Kerygma of the Yahwist," in W. Brueggemann and H. W. Wolff, *Vitality of Old Testament Traditions* (Atlanta: John Knox Press, 1975) 41–66.

7. M. Guinan, *Covenant*, 26–32; M. Weinfeld, "Covenant, Davidic," *IDBS*, 188–192; W. L. Humphreys, *Crisis*, 61–64; M. Tsevat, "King, God as," *IDBS*, 515–516.

8. See R. Gordis, "The Social Background of the Wisdom Literature," *Poets, Prophets and Sages* (Bloomington, Ind.: Indiana University Press, 1971) 160–197; B. Kovacs, "Is There a Class-Ethic in Proverbs?" *Essays in Old Testament Ethics* (J. L. Crenshaw and J. T. Willis, eds.; New York: KTAV, 1974) 173–187; R. N. Whybray, *The Intellectual Tradition in the Old Testament* (New York: W. de Gruyter, 1974) 58–59. More briefly, see D. Ber-

gant, "Blest Are the Not-So-Poor," *Bible Today* #101 (March 1979) 1962–68.

9. Recent years have seen a great renewal of interest in biblical wisdom materials. J. L. Crenshaw, "Wisdom, in the Old Testament," *IDBS*, 952–956; R. B. Y. Scott, *The Way of Wisdom in the Old Testament* (New York: Macmillan, 1971); W. Brueggemann, "Scripture and Ecumenical Life Style," *Int* 24 (1970) 3–19; *In Man We Trust* (Atlanta: John Knox Press,1972).

10. Biblical scholars are realizing the importance and validity of at least two main streams of theology in the Bible—a theology of God's saving acts, and a theology of God's blessings (found in the wisdom, royal and creation traditions). Prominent among these scholars is C. Westermann, *What Does the Old Testament Say About God?* (Atlanta: John Knox, 1979); *Creation* (Philadelphia: Fortress, 1974); *Blessing in the Bible and the Life of the Church* (Philadelphia: Fortress, 1978). See also B. C. Birch and L. L. Rasmussen, *Predicament,* 79–125.

11. This expression is borrowed from W. Brueggemann, *Living Toward a Vision: Biblical Reflections on Shalom* (Philadelphia: United Church Press, 1976) 27–36.

5 The Prophets and the Poor

1. There is a vast literature on the biblical prophets. For a few more recent popular works, see R. B. Y. Scott, *The Relevance of the Prophets* (rev. ed.; New York: Macmillan, 1968), esp. ch. 8, "The Prophets and the Social Order": G. von Rad, *The Message of the Prophets* (New York: Harper and Row, 1965); J. Limburg,

The Prophets and the Powerless (Atlanta: John Knox, 1977). J. Bright, *Covenant and Promise* (Philadelphia: Westminster, 1976), discusses the prophets within the context of the two covenant traditions. W. Brueggemann, *The Prophetic Imagination* (Philadelphia: Fortress Press, 1978), has to be read with a critical eye. While it contains some very exciting material, it tends to compare prophetic thought at its best with royal practice at its worst, and a rather slanted picture emerges.

2. See J. Limburg, *Prophets,* 48–50; R. L. Rohrbaugh, *The Biblical Interpreter: An Agrarian Bible in an Industrial Age* (Philadelphia: Fortress Press, 1978) 53–68.

3. J. Limburg, *Prophets,* 54–75; G. von Rad, *Message,* 102–109; J. Bright, *Covenant and Promise,* 83–87.

4. J. Limburg, *Prophets,* 79–81; G. von Rad, *Message,* 118–144; J. Bright, *Covenant and Promise,* 94–110.

5. G. von Rad, *Message,* 126–144; J. Bright, *Covenant and Promise,* 94, 101; W. L. Humphreys, *Crisis,* 113–114.

6. ". . . neither Amos nor any other of the prophets calls the oppressed to rebellion. The guilty are always attacked directly . . .": H. W. Wolff, *Anthropology,* 195.

6 The Poor and the Pious

1. R. W. Klein, *Israel in Exile: A Theological Interpretation* (Philadelphia: Fortress, 1979), discusses six different theological responses to the crisis of the exile. See also P. Ackroyd, *Exile and Restoration* (Philadelphia: Westminster, 1968).

2. This paradigm of post-exilic tension draws on the ground-breaking work of P. D. Hanson, *The Dawn*

of Apocalyptic (Philadelphia: Fortress, 1975); "Old Testament Apocalyptic Re-examined," *Int* 25 (1971) 454–479; "Apocalypticism," *IDBS*, 28–34. For some discussion of this, see W. Brueggemann, "Trajectories in Old Testament Literature and the Sociology of Ancient Israel," *JBL* 98 (1979) 179, 180, 183. A different view is represented, e.g., by R. E. Brown: "Poverty was the inevitable aftermath of the downfall of the nation. The fact that the rich and the powerful had not been able to prevent the downfall focused the attention of the survivors on God as the only salvation and on poverty as a way of life closer to God than wealth and power. Thus poverty became a religious concept": *Birth of the Messiah* (Garden City, N.Y.: Doubleday, 1977) 351, fn. 36. The problem is simply: How do we explain the transition from sociological condition to religious concept?

3. A. Gelin, *Poor,* 26.

4. L. Keck, "Poor," *IDBS,* 673; G. von Rad, *Old Testament Theology* 1 (New York: Harper and Row, 1962) 400–401; A. George, *GP,* 14–19; A. Gelin, *Poor,* 43–61. W. Brueggemann, "From Hurt to Joy, From Death to Life," *Int* 28 (1974) 10–12, discusses some theories on the speakers of the psalms of lament. In the same way, various theories have been proposed concerning the identity of the "enemies" in these psalms. See, briefly, B. Anderson, *Out of the Depths: The Psalms Speak for Us Today* (Philadelphia: Westminster, 1974) 58–60.

7 The Community of Qumran

1. A great deal has been written about Qumran and the Dead Sea Scrolls. Especially useful are F. M. Cross, *The Ancient Library of Qumran* (rev. ed; Garden

City, N.Y.: Doubleday, 1961); J. Milik, *Ten Years of Discovery in the Wilderness of Judea* (*Studies in Biblical Theology* No. 26; London: SCM Press, 1959); G. Vermes, *The Dead Sea Scrolls, Qumran in Perspective* (Cleveland, Ohio: Collins-World, 1977).

2. The page references are to G. Vermes, *The Dead Sea Scrolls in English* (2nd edition; New York: Penguin Books, 1975).

3. L. Keck, "Poor," *IDBS,* 673. J. Fitzmyer calls it "a rare, non-technical usage" in "Jewish Christianity in Acts in the Light of the Qumran Scrolls," *Essays on the Semitic Background of the New Testament* (Sources for Biblical Study 5; Missoula, Mont.: Scholars Press, 1974) 288.

4. On the history of the sect, see G. Vermes, *The Dead Sea Scrolls,* 136–162.

5. F. M. Cross, *Ancient Library,* 84. "The Essene 'poor' were in some sense an 'artificial' poor, the elite of (the) desert who shared their goods": 241.

6. F. M. Cross, *Ancient Library,* 60, fn. 15; J. Milik, *Ten Years,* 102, fn. 1.

8 Jesus

1. The difficulties of theological language are often discussed today. See, for example, L. Gilkey, *Catholicism Confronts Modernity* (New York: Seabury Press, 1975), 84–104. On the problem in general, see I. Ramsey, *Religious Language* (New York: Macmillan, 1957).

2. For a fuller discussion of these Pauline texts, see P. Seidensticker, *GP,* 92–95, 107–112.

3. That Jesus was an itinerant preacher has been a consensus among scholars. F. H. Borsch, "Jesus, the Wandering Preacher?" *What About the New Testament?*

(M. Hooker and C. Hickling, eds; London: SCM Press, 1975) 45–63, surveys this consensus and then strongly challenges it. The activity of the "wandering charismatics" has been raised from a new angle by G. Theissen, *The Sociology of Early Palestinian Christianity* (Philadelphia: Fortress Press, 1975). Serious methodological questions have been raised here—see B. Malina, *CBQ* 41 (1979) 176–178, and R. Kraemer, *JBL* 98 (1979) 436–438—so at this time the question of Jesus as itinerant preacher would seem to be moot.

4. The medieval controversy over the poverty and purse of Jesus was heavily influenced by the presuppositions of the age. See S. Clausen, "Poverty Controversy," *NCE* 11, 651–653. On the missionary instructions to "take nothing for the journey," two observations are in order. (1) The disciples are to depend on the hospitality of those to whom they preach. The Semitic practice of hospitality is a far cry from begging. (2) After the death and resurrection of Jesus, the disciples can expect no longer hospitality but hostility. With this change of situation, Jesus' instructions change (Lk 22:35). See J. Dupont, *GP*, 27–29.

5. L. Keck, "Poor," *IDBS*, 673.

6. B. Rigaux, *GP*, 144; M. Hengel, *Property*, 26–28. J. B. Metz, *Poverty of Spirit* (New York: Paulist Press, 1968) 38: ". . . the *poverty of misery and neediness*. Jesus was no stranger to this poverty either. He was a beggar, knocking on men's doors . . ." This is a rather questionable section in an otherwise fine little book.

7. In this section, I depend heavily on J. Dupont, *GP*, 34–41. Basic to understanding Jesus and his work is his preaching to the poor. See, e.g., H. Küng, *On Being a Christian* (New York: Wallaby Books, 1978) 265–271; J. Jeremias, *New Testament Theology* (New York:

Chas. Scribner's Sons, 1971) 108–121; G. Bornkamm, *Jesus of Nazareth* (New York: Harper and Row, 1956) 75–81; W. Kaspar, *Jesus the Christ* (New York: Paulist Press, 1976) 83–88.

8. So, e.g., A. Gelin, *Poor,* 107–108.

9. As an apocalyptic movement, early Christianity attracted large numbers of the poor and the outcasts of society. See J. Gager, *Kingdom and Community* (Englewood Cliffs, N.J.: Prentice-Hall, 1975) 24–25.

10 J.J. Donahue, "Tax Collectors and Sinners," *CBQ* 33 (1971) 39–61. These toll collectors were indeed marginal and despised in society, but not because they were poor. Rather, it was because of the way in which they had become rich.

11. Recent study has shown that the specific function of a parable is to upset the presuppositions that a group shares. See D. Crossan, *The Dark Interval* (Niles, Ill.: Argus, 1975) 90–93, 101–104; *In Parables* (New York: Harper and Row, 1973) 68–69.

9 The Early Christian Community

1. In this section, I again rely on J. Dupont, *GP,* 29–34. See also J. Murphy-O'Connor, *Religious Life,* 42–43.

2. In addition to Dupont, see, e.g., R. Dillon, "The Acts of the Apostles," *JBC* 45:23–24. It would be going too far, however, to regard these summaries of Luke as being totally fictitious. See R. E. Brown, *Birth,* 354, fn. 46. The early Church did indeed become renowned for its charitable activity. See J. Gager, *Kingdom,* 131, 146 fn. 73.

3. Luke has added to his presentation of the Greek ideal of friendship the Old Testament expectation (Dt 15:4) which promised that when God's commands are

perfectly fulfilled, there will be no more need in the land. If people truly live the covenant, poverty will cease to be. In addition to Dupont, see R. Karris, *What Are They Saying About Luke-Acts?* (New York: Paulist Press, 1979) 88–89, 92–94, 98; B. C. Birch and L. L. Rasmussen, *Bible and Ethics,* 181; *Predicament,* 86–87. Some have seen here influence from the Essene community of Qumran. See, for example, J. Fitzmyer, "Jewish Christianity," 284–288.

4. P. Seidensticker, *GP,* 86–88; M. Hengel, *Property and Riches,* 36.

5. "The communities founded by Paul were certainly not well-to-do": M. Hengel, *Property and Riches,* 36; ". . . the Pauline communities are to be ranked . . . in the category of the well-off middle class": P. Seidensticker, *GP,* 99–100; "The Pauline communities were of diverse economic status": L. Keck, "Poor," *IDBS,* 674.

6. This position is argued especially by F. B. Craddock, "The Poverty of Christ, An Investigation of 2 Cor 8:19," *Int* 22 (1968) 158–170. See also P. Seidensticker, *GP,* 92–95, and J. Dupont, *GP,* 49–50. Special difficulties attach to the question of Paul's collection for the "poor among the saints in Jerusalem" (Acts 11:29; 24:17; Rom 15:25–27; 1 Cor 16:1–4; 2 Cor 8—9; Gal 2:10). When and how often did it take place? Was "the poor" a technical title for the Jerusalem church as it may have been for Qumran? See P. Seidensticker, *GP,* 88–92; L. Keck, "Poor," *IDBS,* 674–675, and the literature cited there.

7. M. Hengel, *Property and Riches,* 54–59; P. Seidensticker, *GP,* 109–110, 114.

8. The most thorough study of this pericope is that of S. Légasse, *L'Appel du riche* (Paris: Beauchesne, 1966); he summarizes his conclusions in his article in

GP, 53–80. On the danger of riches, see also J. Dupont, *GP*, 46–49; J. Murphy-O'Connor, *Religious Life*, 44–46; D. Malone, "Riches and Discipleship, Mark 10:23–31," *Biblical Theology Bulletin* 9 (1979) 78–88.

9. J. Murphy-O'Connor, *Religious Life*, 45. "Possessions are not evil *in se*, but can be used for good. They do, however, have the potential to become demonic. In the context of Jesus' proclamation on the Kingdom, the question addressed is not wealth *per se*, but the priority of values that is being examined. Seeking the Kingdom of God takes priority over all attachments and use of good things of this world": D. Malone, "Riches and Discipleship," 85.

10. On this pericope, see J. Dupont, "Renoncer a tous ses biens (Luc 14:33)," *NRT* 93 (1971) 561–582. On the obstacles that family ties presented to conversion, see J. Gager, *Kingdom*, 131.

11. "Luke ranks high in popular esteem as the champion of the poor. More aptly, he might be called the conscience of the rich": R. Karris, *Invitation to Luke* (Garden City, N.Y.: Doubleday, 1977) 16. By the same author, see *What Are They Saying?* 84–104; "Poor and Rich: The Lukan *Sitz-im-Leben*," *Perspectives on Luke-Acts* (C. H. Talbert, ed.; Association of Baptist Professors of Religion, 1978) 112–125.

12. L. Keck, "Poor," *IDBS*, 674.

10 Gospel Poverty: Witness to the Risen Christ

1. (Maryknoll, N.Y.: Orbis Books, 1973) 299.

2. "... others make a consistent effort to strip themselves of worldly goods in order to attain the state of insecurity that characterizes the truly poor. . . . (This) rests on a radical misunderstanding of the gospel mes-

sage": J. Murphy-O'Connor, *Religious Life,* 41. F. B. Craddock, in commenting on 2 Cor 8:19, remarks, "Such exaltation of the condition of poverty as a most blessed state, as though a man's life consisted in the abundance of things he did *not* possess, has had a long and widespread acceptance in the Church. . . . This misplaced accent is a cheapening of the Christ-event and a misunderstanding of Paul": "Poverty of Christ," 162.

3. A. Gelin, *Poor,* 91–98; R. E. Brown, *Birth,* 346–366.

4. *Liberation,* 299. We should note that Gutierrez goes on to reject the biblical idea of poverty-scandal as "subtly deceptive" and of spiritual poverty as "partial and insufficient," and wants to "move forward toward a better understanding of the Christian witness of poverty." Then he asks, "How are we . . . to understand the evangelical meaning of the witness of a real, material, concrete poverty?" Having rejected the biblical, evangelical teaching, where does Gutierrez derive his conviction that there is in fact an "evangelical meaning of . . . real, material, concrete poverty"? This seems a curious ideological sleight of hand (all quotes, p. 299).

5. Real human need exists on a variety of levels—physical, psychological, social, spiritual. For a preliminary discussion, see S. Jourard, *Healthy Personality* (New York: Macmillan, 1974) 72–94.